Life and Holiness

Life and Holiness

THOMAS MERTON

Introduction by Henri J. M. Nouwen

IMAGE BOOKS
DOUBLEDAY
NEW YORK LONDON TORONTO SYDNEY AUCKLAND

IN MEMORIAM: LOUIS MASSIGNON 1883-1962.

CONTENTS

INTRODUCTION

TO THE 1996 EDITION

Life and Holiness was written by Thomas Merton more than thirty years ago. It is a straightforward, clear, intelligent, and very convincing statement about being a Christian.

Reading this book brought back to mind my one and only encounter with Merton in a brief meeting during a visit I made to the Abbey of Gethsemani. There was a no-nonsense quality about him. Direct, open, unsentimental, and always with a twinkle in his eye. That's how Merton was. That's how this book is.

I often wonder: "What book do I give to someone who wants to know what being-a-Christian looks like?" This is definitely the book. It is not a book about doctrines or dogmas but about the life in Christ. It could have been called *Christ in the Center* because in everything Merton says about life and holiness, he places Christ in the center. He says: ". . . faith is *the rejection of everything that is not Christ, in order that all life, all truth, all hope, all reality may be sought and found in Christ.*" In its great simplicity, this is a radical book. It calls for a total dedication and a total commitment.

Reading this book brings me in touch with what is permanent, lasting, and "of God." So much has happened since Merton's death that it nearly seems that all the solid ground has vanished under our feet and we have become like people trying to cross a lake by jumping from one piece of drifting ice to another. What we desire is something that gives us a solid footing, something we can trust, something that is true. Merton tells us: That something is someone! It is Jesus who guides us through this valley of darkness by giving us his own spirit, his own life, his own love. Because of its radical focus on Christ, this book is a classic, not bound to the passing intellectual fashion of the time. It is as spiritually nourishing now as when it was first written.

In his autobiography *The Seven Storey Mountain*, Merton remembers a conversation with his friend Bob Lax. While walking on Sixth Avenue in New York City one spring evening, Bob Lax suddenly turned around and asked him:

LAX: What do you want to be, anyway?

MERTON: I don't know; I guess what I want is to be a good Catholic.

LAX: What do you mean, you want to be a good Catholic? . . . What you should say . . . is that you want to be a saint.

MERTON: How do you expect me to become a saint?

LAX: By wanting to.

MERTON: I can't be a saint. I can't be a saint . . .

LAX: All that is necessary to be a saint is to want to be one. Don't you believe that God will make you what He created you to be if you consent to let Him do it? All you have to do is desire it.*

* From*The Seven Storey Mountain*, New York: Harcourt, Brace and Co., 1948, 1978 (New American Library, 1961), pp. 237–38.

Merton realizes the power of his friend's challenge. Many years later, after twenty-two years of life as a Trappist monk, he writes this basic and very practical book about becoming a saint. He surely knew what he was writing about! He writes with humility and conviction, with gentleness and force, with humor and wisdom.

Merton died twenty-seven years ago. His friend Bob Lax now lives on Patmos. I am sure that Bob will smile with gratitude when he sees this book again and remembers his walk with Tom long, long ago!

Henri J. M. Nouwen
Toronto, 1996

INTRODUCTION

This is intended to be a very simple book, an elementary treatment of a few basic ideas in Christian spirituality. Hence it should be useful to any Christian, and indeed to anyone who wants to acquaint himself with some principles of the interior life as it is understood in the Catholic Church. Nothing is here said of such subjects as "contemplation" or even "mental prayer." And yet the book emphasizes what is at once the most common and the most mysterious aspect in the Christian life: grace, the power and the light of God in us, purifying our hearts, transforming us in Christ, making us true sons of God, enabling us to act in the world as his instruments for the good of all men and for his glory.

This is therefore a meditation on some fundamental themes appropriate to the active life. It must be said at once that the active life is essential to every Christian. Clearly the active life must mean more than the life which is led in religious institutes of men and women who teach, care for the sick, and so on. (When one is talking of the "active life" as opposed to the "contemplative life," this is the usual reference.) Here action is not looked at in opposition to contemplation, but as an expression of charity and as a necessary consequence of union with God by baptism.

The active life is the participation of the Christian in the Church's mission on earth, whether it means bringing to other men the message of the Gospel, or administering the sacraments, or performing works of mercy, or cooperating in the world-wide efforts for the spiritual renewal of society and the establishment of that peace and order without which the human race cannot achieve its destiny. Even the cloistered "contemplative" is inevitably implicated in the crises and problems of the society in which he is still a member (since he participates in its benefits and shares its responsibilities). Even he must to some extent participate "actively" in the Church's work, not only by prayer and holiness, but by understanding and concern.

Even in contemplative monasteries productive work is essential to the life of the community, and such work generally represents a service to society at large. Even contemplatives are, then, implicated in the economy of their nation. It is right that they should understand the nature of their service, and some of its implications. This is all the more true when the monastery offers to men the "service"—a very essential one indeed—of shelter and recollection during times of spiritual retreat.

But I have declared that this book is not to be about contemplatives. Let it suffice to say that all Christians should be concerned with the "active life" as it is treated here: the life which, in response to divine grace and in union with the visible authority of the Church, devotes its efforts to the spiritual and material development of the whole human community.

This does not mean that this book intends to treat of specific techniques appropriate to Christian action in the world. It is concerned rather with the life of grace from which all valid Christian action must spring. If the Christian life is like a vine, then this book has more to say about the root system than about the leaves and the fruits.

Is it strange that in this book on the active life the emphasis is not on energy and will-power and action so much as on grace, and interiority? No, for these are the true principles of supernatural activity. An activity that is based on the frenzies and impulsions of human ambition is a delusion and an obstacle to grace. It gets in the way of God's will, and it creates more problems than it solves. We must learn to distinguish between the pseudo spirituality of activism and the true vitality and energy of Christian action guided by the Spirit. At the same time we must not create a split in the Christian life by assuming that all activity is somehow dangerous to the spiritual life. The spiritual life is not a life of quiet withdrawal, a hothouse growth of artificial ascetic practices beyond the reach of people living ordinary lives. It is in the ordinary duties and labors of life that the Christian can and should develop his spiritual union with God.

This is no new principle. But it is perhaps not often easy to apply in practice. A writer or preacher who assumes that it is very easy may seriously mislead those who try to follow his advice. Work in a normal, healthy human context, work with a sane and moderate human measure, integrated in a productive social milieu, is by itself capable of contributing much to the spiritual life. But work that is disordered, irrational, unproductive, dominated by the exhausting frenzies and wastefulness of a world-wide struggle for power and wealth, is not necessarily going to make a valid contribution to the spiritual lives of all those engaged in it. Hence it is important to consider the nature of work and its place in the Christian life.

This book devotes some pages to this subject, though of course the treatment is by no means complete. Whole areas of vexation and confusion have been ignored. I have thought it sufficient to indicate briefly that one's daily work is an all important element in the spiritual life, and that for work to be truly sanctifying the Christian must not only offer it to God in a mental and subjective effort of will, but must strive to integrate it in the whole pattern of Christian striving for order and peace in the world. The work of each Christian must be not only honest and decent, it must not only be productive, but it should contribute a positive service to human society.

It should have a part in the general striving of all men for a peaceful and well-ordered civilization in this world, for in that way it best helps us to prepare for the next world.

The Christian striving for holiness (and the striving for holiness remains an essential of the Christian life) must then be placed today within the context of the Church's action on the threshold of a new age. It is not permissible to delude ourselves with a retreat into a vanished past. Holiness is not and never has been a mere escape from responsibility and from participation in the fundamental task of man to live justly and productively in community with his fellow men.

Pope John XXIII opened the Vatican Council on October 11, 1962, with these profoundly stirring words: "In the present order of things, divine providence is leading us to a new order of human relations which by men's efforts and even beyond their expectations are directed toward the fulfillment of God's superior and inscrutable designs."

Christian holiness in our age means more than ever the awareness of our common responsibility to cooperate with the mysterious designs of God for the human race. This awareness will be illusory unless it is enlightened by divine grace, strengthened by generous effort, and sought in collaboration not only with the authorities of the Church but with all men of good will who are sincerely working for the temporal and spiritual good of the human race.

THOMAS MERTON

I. CHRISTIAN IDEALS

CALLED OUT OF DARKNESS

Every baptized Christian is obliged by his baptismal promises to renounce sin and to give himself completely, without compromise, to Christ, in order that he may fulfill his vocation, save his soul, enter into the mystery of God, and there find himself perfectly "in the light of Christ."

As St. Paul reminds us (1 Cor. 6:19), we are "not our own." We belong entirely to Christ. His Spirit has taken possession of us at baptism. We are the Temples of the Holy Spirit. Our thoughts, our actions, our desires, are by rights more his than our own. But we have to struggle to ensure that God always receives from us what we owe him by right. If we do not labor to overcome our natural weakness, our disordered and selfish passions, what belongs to God in us will be withdrawn from the sanctifying power of his love and will be corrupted by selfishness, blinded by irrational desire, hardened by pride, and will eventually plunge into the abyss of moral nonentity which is called sin.

Sin is the refusal of spiritual life, the rejection of the inner order and peace that come from our union with the divine will. In a word, sin is the refusal of God's will and of his love. It is not only a refusal to "do" this or that thing willed by God, or a determination to do what he forbids. It is more radically a refusal to be what we are, a rejection of our mysterious, contingent, spiritual reality hidden in the very mystery of God. Sin is our refusal to be what we were created to be—sons of God, images of God. Ultimately sin, while seeming to be an assertion of freedom, is a flight from the freedom and the responsibility of divine sonship.

Every Christian is therefore called to sanctity and union with Christ, by keeping the commandments of God. Some, however, with special vocations have contracted a more solemn obligation by religious vows, and have bound themselves to take the basic Christian vocation to holiness especially seriously. They have promised to make use of certain definite and more efficacious means to "be perfect"—the evangelical counsels. They obligate themselves to be poor, chaste, and obedient, thereby renouncing their own wills, denying themselves, and liberating themselves from mundane attachments in order to give themselves even more perfectly to Christ. For them, sanctity is not simply something that is sought as an ultimate end: sanctity is their "profession"—they have no other job in life than to be saints, and everything is subordinated to this end, which is primary and immediate for them.

Nevertheless, the fact that religious and clerics have a professional obligation to strive for holiness must be properly understood. It does not imply that they alone are fully Christians, as if the laity were in some sense less truly Christian and less fully members of Christ than they. St. John Chrysostom who, in his youth, came close to believing that one could not be saved unless he fled to the desert, recognized in later life, as bishop of Antioch and then of Constantinople, that all the members of Christ are called to holiness by the very fact that they are his members. There is only *one* morality, one holiness for the Christian—that proposed to all in the Gospels. The lay state is necessarily good and holy, since the New Testament leaves us free to choose it. Nor is the lay state one in which it is sufficient to maintain a kind of static and minimal holiness, simply by "avoiding sin." Sometimes the difference between the states of life is so distorted and oversimplified in the minds of Christians that they seem to think that while priests, monks, and nuns are obliged to grow and make progress in perfection, the layman is expected only to keep in the state of grace and, by clinging as it were to the cassock of the priest, to let himself be drawn into heaven by specialists who alone are called to "perfection."

St. John Chrysostom points out that the mere fact that the life of the monk is more austere and more difficult should not make us think that Christian holiness is principally a matter of *difficulty*. This would lead to the false conclusion that because salvation seems less arduous for the layman it is also in some strange way less truly salvation. On the contrary, says Chrysostom, "God has not treated us [laypeople and secular clergy] with such severity as to demand of us monastic austerities as a matter of duty. He has left to all a free choice [in the matter of his counsels]. One must be chaste in marriage, one must be temperate in meals . . . You are not ordered to renounce your possessions. God only commands you not to steal, and to share your property with those who lack what they need" (*Commentary on I Corinthians*, ix, 2).

In other words, the ordinary temperance, justice, and charity which every Christian must practice, are sanctifying in the same way as the virginity and poverty of the nun. It is true that the life of the consecrated religious has a greater dignity and a greater intrinsic perfection. The religious takes on a more radical and more total commitment to love God and his fellow man. But this must not be understood to mean that the life of the lay person is downgraded to the point of insignificance. On the contrary, we must come to recognize that the married state is also most sanctifying by its very nature, and it may, accidentally, imply sacrifices and a self-forgetfulness that, in particular cases, would be even more effective than the sacrifices of religious life. He who in *actual fact* loves more perfectly will be closer to God, whether or not he happens to be a layman.

Hence St. Chrysostom again protests against the error that monks alone need to strive for perfection, while lay people need only avoid hell. On the contrary, both lay people and monks have to lead a very positive and constructive Christian life of virtue. It is not sufficient for the tree to remain alive, it must also bear fruit. "It is not enough to leave Egypt," he says, "one must also travel to the promised Land" (*Homily xvi on Ephesians*). At the same time, even the perfect practice of one or other of the counsels, such as virginity, would be meaningless if the one practicing it lacked the more elementary and universal virtues of justice and charity. He says: "It is vain for you to fast and sleep on the ground, to eat ashes and to weep without ceasing. If you are no use to anybody else, you are doing nothing of any importance" (*Homily vi on Titus*). "Though you are a virgin you will be cast out of the bridal chamber if you do not give alms" (*Homily lxxvii on Matthew*). Nevertheless the monks have their important part to play in the Church. Their prayers and sanctity are of irreplaceable value to the whole Church. Their example teaches the layman to live also as a "stranger and pilgrim on this earth," detached from material things, and preserving his Christian freedom in the midst of the vain agitation of the cities, because he seeks in all things only to please Christ and to serve him in his fellow man.

In short, according to Chrysostom, "The beatitudes pronounced by Christ cannot possibly be reserved for the use of monks alone, for that would be the ruin of the universe." (For Chrysostom's doctrine on the monastic and lay state, see J.-M. Leroux, "Monachisme et communauté chrétienne d'après S. Jean Chrysostome," in *Théologie de la vie monastique* [Paris, 1961], pp. 143 ff.)

But in fact, all of us who have been baptized in Christ and have "put on Christ" as a new identity, are bound to be holy as he is holy. We are bound to live worthy lives, and our actions should bear witness to our union with him. He should manifest his presence in us and through us. Though the reminder may make us blush, we have to recognize that these solemn words of Christ are addressed to us:

"You are the light of the world. A city set on a mountain cannot be hidden. Neither do men light a lamp and put it under a measure, but upon the lampstand, so as to give light to all in the house. Even so let your light shine before men, in order that they may see your good works and give glory to your Father in heaven" (Mt. 5:14-16).

The Fathers of the Church, particularly Clement of Alexandria, believed that the "light" in man is his divine sonship, the Word living in him. They therefore taught that the whole of the Christian life was summed up in a service of God which was not only a matter of outward worship, but of "cherishing that which is divine in ourselves by means of unremitting charity" (*Stromata vii.* 1). Clement adds that Christ himself teaches us the way of perfection and that the whole Christian life is a course of spiritual education conducted by the One Master, through his Holy Spirit. In writing this, he was addressing himself to *laymen*.

We are supposed to be the light of the world. We are supposed to be a light to ourselves and to others. That may well be what accounts for the fact that the world is in darkness! What then is meant by the light of Christ in our lives? What is "holiness"? What is divine sonship? Are we really seriously supposed to be saints? Can a man even desire such a thing without making a complete fool of himself in the eyes of everyone else? Is it not presumptuous? Is such a thing even possible at all? To tell the truth, many lay people and even a good many religious do not believe, in practice, that sanctity is possible for them. Is this just plain common sense? Is it perhaps humility? Or is it defection, defeatism, and despair?

If we are called by God to holiness of life, and if holiness is beyond our natural power to achieve (which it certainly is) then it follows that God himself must give us the light, the strength, and the courage to fulfill the task he requires of us. He will certainly give us the grace we need. If we do not become saints it is because we do not avail ourselves of his gift.

However, we must be careful not to oversimplify this delicate problem. We must not glibly assume that the failure of Christians to be perfect always is due to bad will, to laziness, or to crass sinfulness. Rather it is due to confusion, to blindness, to weakness, and to misunderstanding. We do not really appreciate the meaning and the greatness of our vocation. We do not know how to value the "unfathomable riches of Christ" (Eph. 3:9). The mystery of God, of the divine redemption and of his infinite mercy is generally nebulous and unreal even to "men of faith." Hence we do not have the courage or the strength to respond to our vocation in all its depth. We unconsciously falsify it, distort its true perspectives, and reduce our Christian life to a kind of genteel and social propriety. In such an event Christian "perfection" no longer consists in the arduous and strange fidelity of the spirit to grace in the darkness of the night of faith. It becomes, in practice, a respectable conformity to what is commonly accepted as "good" in the society in which we live. The stress is then placed on exterior signs of respectability.

Certainly this exteriority must not automatically be dismissed as pharisaism, itself altogether too facile a cliché. There may indeed be much real moral goodness in this kind of respectability. Good intentions are not lost in the sight of God. However, there will always be a certain lack of depth and a definite one-sidedness, an incompleteness that will make it impossible for such persons to attain to the full likeness of Christ, unless they can transcend the limitations of their social group by making the sacrifices demanded of them by the Spirit of Christ, sacrifices which may estrange them from certain of their fellows and force upon them decisions of a lonely and terrible responsibility.

The way of Christian holiness is, in any case, hard and austere. We must fast and pray. We must embrace hardship and sacrifice, for the love of Christ, and in order to improve the condition of man on earth. We may not merely enjoy the good things of life ourselves, occasionally "purifying our intention" to make sure that we are doing it all "for God." Such purely abstract and mental operations are only a pitiful excuse for mediocrity. They do not justify us in the sight of God. It is not enough to make pious gestures. Our love of God and of man cannot be merely symbolic, it has to be completely real. It is not just a mental operation, but the gift and commitment of our inmost self.

Obviously, this means going a little further than the vapid preachments of that popular religion which has led some people to believe that a "religious revival" is taking place among us. Let us not be too sure of that! The mere fact that men are frightened and insecure, that they grasp at optimistic slogans, run more frequently to Church, and seek to pacify their troubled souls by cheerful and humanitarian maxims, is surely no indication that our society is becoming "religious." In fact, it may be a symptom of spiritual sickness. It is certainly a good thing to be aware of our symptoms, but that does not justify our palliating them with quack medicines.

Let us not therefore delude ourselves with easy and infantile conceptions of holiness.

It is unfortunately quite possible that a superficial religiosity, without deep roots and without fruitful relation to the needs of men and of society, may turn out in the end to be an evasion of imperative religious obligations. Our time needs more than devout, Church-going people who avoid serious wrongs (or at least the wrongs that are easily recognized for what they are) but who seldom do anything constructive or positively good. It is not enough to be outwardly respectable. On the contrary, mere external respectability, without deeper or more positive moral values, brings discredit upon the Christian faith.

The experience of twentieth-century dictatorships has shown that it is possible for some Christians to live and work in a shockingly unjust society, closing their eyes to all kinds of evil and indeed perhaps participating in that evil at least by default, concerned only with their own compartmentalized life of piety, closed off from everything else on the face of the earth. Clearly, such a poor excuse for religion actually contributes to blindness and moral insensitivity, and in the long run it leads to the death of Christianity in whole nations or whole areas of society. It is this no doubt that has led to the great modern problem of the Church: the loss of the working class.

That is why it is perhaps advisable to speak of "holiness" rather than "perfection." A "holy" person is one who is sanctified by the presence and action of God in him. He is "holy" because he lives so deeply immersed in the life, the faith, and the charity of the "holy Church" that she manifests her sanctity in and through him. But if one concentrates on "perfection" he is likely to have a more subtly egoistic attitude. He may run the risk of wishing to contemplate himself as a superior being, complete and adorned with every virtue, in isolation from all others and in pleasing contrast to them. The idea of "holiness" seems to imply something of communion and solidarity in a "holy People of God." The notion of "spiritual perfection" is appropriate rather to a philosopher who, by the knowledge and practice of esoteric disciplines, unconcerned with the needs and desires of other men, has arrived at a state of tranquillity where passions no longer trouble his pure soul.

This is not the Christian idea of holiness.

THE PLASTER SAINT

A very wise piece of advice, which St. Benedict gives to monks in his Rule, is that they should not desire to be called saints before they are holy, but that they should first become saints in order that their reputation for holiness may be based on reality. This brings out the great difference between real spiritual perfection and man's idea of perfection. Or perhaps one might say, more accurately, the difference between sanctity and narcissism.

The popular idea of a "saint" is, of course, quite naturally based on the sanctity which is presented for our veneration, in heroic men and women, by the Church. There is nothing surprising in the fact that the saints quickly become stereotyped in the mind of the average Christian, and everyone, on reflection, will easily admit that the stereotype tends to be unreal. The conventions of hagiography have usually accentuated the unreality of the picture, and pious art has, in most cases, successfully completed the work. In this way, the Christian who devotes himself to the pursuit of holiness unconsciously tends to reproduce in himself some features of the popular stereotyped image. Or rather, since it is fortunately difficult to succeed in this enterprise, he imagines himself in some sense obliged to follow the pattern, as if it were really a model proposed for his imitation by the Church herself, instead of a purely conventional and popular caricature of a mysterious reality—the Christlikeness of the saints.

The stereotyped image is easy to sketch out here: it is essentially an image without the slightest moral flaw. The saint, if he ever sinned at all, eventually became impeccable after a perfect conversion. Impeccability not being quite enough, he is raised beyond the faintest possibility of feeling temptation. Of course he is tempted, but temptation provides no difficulties. He always has the absolute and heroic answer. He flings himself into fire, ice water or briers rather than even face a remote occasion of sin. His intentions are always the noblest. His words are always the most edifying clichés, fitting the situation with a devastating obviousness that silences even the thought of dialogue. Indeed, the "perfect" in this fearsome sense are elevated above the necessity or even the capacity for a fully human dialogue with their fellow men. They are without humor as they are without wonder, without feeling and without interest in the common affairs of mankind. Yet of course they always rush to the scene with the precise act of virtue called for by every situation. They are always there kissing the leper's sores at the very moment when the king and his noble attendants come around the corner and stop in their tracks, mute in admiration. . . .

There is no one who will not smile at the naïve beginner who trustingly embarks upon the reproduction of this kind of image in his life. He will always be told to face reality; yet when he is reminded of the sorry facts of life, do we not often assume, secretly, that he is, after all, right? Sanctity is indeed a cult of the *absolute*. It is intransigent, and does not even consider compromise. Do we not really, in our hearts, mean by this that the miracle of sanctity is somehow not only supernatural but even inhuman? Do we not, as a matter of fact, equate the supernatural with a flat denial of the human? Are not nature and grace diametrically opposed? Does not sanctity mean the absolute rejection and renunciation of all that accords with nature?

If we think this, we are in practice admitting the reality of the stereotyped image, and in that case we have no alternative than to assume that this is the model that is supposed to be realized by the perfect Christian. By what right, then, do we dissuade people from seeking to realize what is in all truth their model?

The fact is that our concept of sanctity is ambiguous and obscure, and this is perhaps because our concept of grace and the supernatural is itself confused. The adage that grace "builds on nature" is by no means a cliché that was devised to excuse half measures in the spiritual life. It is the strict truth, and until we realize that before a man can become a saint he must first of all be a *man* in all the humanity and fragility of man's actual condition, we will never be able to understand the meaning of the word "saint." Not only were all the saints perfectly human, not only did their sanctity enrich and deepen their humanity, but the Holiest of all the Saints, the Incarnate Word, Jesus Christ, was himself the most deeply and perfectly human being who ever lived on the face of the earth. We must remember that human nature was, in him, quite perfect, and at the same time completely like our own frail and suffering nature in all things except sin. Now what is the "supernatural" if not the economy of our salvation in and through the Incarnate Word?

If we are to be "perfect" as Christ is perfect, we must strive to be as perfectly human as he, in order that he may unite us with his divine being and share with us his sonship of the heavenly Father. Hence sanctity is not a matter of being *less* human, but *more* human than other men. This implies a greater capacity for concern, for suffering, for understanding, for sympathy, and also for humor, for joy, for appreciation of the good and beautiful things of life. It follows that a pretended "way of perfection" that simply destroys or frustrates human values precisely because they are human, and in order to set oneself apart from the rest of men as an object of wonder, is doomed to be nothing but a caricature. And such caricaturing of sanctity is indeed a sin against faith in the

Incarnation. It shows contempt for the humanity for which Christ did not hesitate to die on the cross.

However, we must be careful not to confuse genuinely human values with the rather less than human values that come to be accepted in a disordered society. In actual fact, we are suffering more from the distortion and underdevelopment of our deepest human tendencies than from a superabundance of animal instincts. That is why the stern asceticism that was devised to control violent passions may do more harm than good when it is applied to a person whose emotions have never properly matured and whose instinctual life is suffering from weakness and disorder.

We must reflect more deeply than we do on the effect of modern technological life upon the emotional and instinctual development of man. It is quite possible that the person whose life is divided between tending a machine and watching TV is sooner or later going to suffer a radical deprivation in his nature and humanity.

Holiness presupposes not only a normal human intelligence, properly developed and formed by Christian education, a normal human will, a trained liberty capable of self-commitment and self-oblation, but even before all this it presupposes sound and ordered human emotions. Grace builds on nature not by suppressing instinct but by healing and elevating it to a spiritual level. There must always be a proper place for healthy, instinctive spontaneity in the Christian life. The emotions and instincts of man were at work in the sacred humanity of Christ Our Lord: He showed in all things a sensitive and warmly responsive humanness. The Christian who wants to imitate his Master must learn to do so not by imposing a crude and violent control on his emotions (and in most cases his efforts to do so will be a failure) but by letting grace form and develop his emotional life in the service of charity.

Jesus asked the Pharisees: "How can you believe, who

seek glory one from another?" (Jn. 5:44). To seek a heroicity of virtue that will give us glory in the eyes of other men is in reality to weaken our faith. The true saint is not one who has become convinced that he himself is holy, but one who is overwhelmed by the realization that God, and God alone, is holy. He is so awestruck with the reality of the divine holiness that he begins to see it everywhere. Eventually, he may be able to see it in himself too: but surely he will see it there last of all, because in himself he will continue to experience the nothingness, the pseudo reality of egoism and sin. Yet even in the darkness of our disposition to evil shines the presence and the mercy of the divine Saviour. The saint is capable, as Dostoievsky said, of loving others even in their sin. For what he sees in all things and in all men is the object of the divine compassion.

The saint, then, seeks not his own glory but the glory of God. And in order that God may be glorified in all things, the saint wishes himself to be nothing but a pure instrument of the divine will. He wants himself to be simply a window through which God's mercy shines on the world. And for this he strives to be holy. He strives to practice virtue heroically, not in order to be known as a virtuous and holy man, but in order that the goodness of God may never be obscured by any selfish act of his.

Hence it is that he who loves God, and seeks the glory of God, seeks to become, by God's grace, perfect in love, as the "heavenly Father is perfect" (Mt. 5:48).

IDEAS AND REALITY

It is always a little foolish to try to set down, in a few clear formulas, the essence of Christian perfection. Sometimes this has to be done. But whenever we try to do it, we must remind ourselves that we do not grasp the meaning of the words right away, and we must take steps to avoid creating the impression that sanctity can be easily achieved by following some simple formula. "Becoming a saint" is not just a matter of picking out a suitable recipe and cooking up the various ingredients of the Christian life according to a formula which pleases our own taste. Yet this is what some spiritual books would sometimes seem to do. And there are always those "holy souls" who have discovered a new method, which sums it all up, and which will henceforth make the whole thing very simple for everyone.

It is of course natural to look for a simple method of solving all spiritual problems. Traditionally, the most fundamental question a man can ask is "What must we do?" (Acts 2:37). The Christian answer, "Repent, be baptized, . . . to have your sins forgiven; then you will receive the Holy Spirit" (38), is not the exposition of a "method" or a technique. On the contrary, what St. Peter was thus telling the hearers of his first sermon on the first Pentecost, was that salvation did not consist in following a method so much as in becoming a member of the People of God, the Body of Christ, and living as a member of that Body, with the life of that People, which is a life of love. But love in this context is not simply a question of affectivity and benign interior dispositions.

The love that is essential for true Christian life involves participation in all the struggles, problems, and aspirations of the Church. To love is to be fully committed to the Church's work of salvation, the renewal and dedication of man and his society to God. No Christian can remain unconcerned in this work. Today, the dimensions of the task are as wide as the world itself.

Nevertheless, the task begins within each Christian soul. We cannot bring hope and redemption to others unless we are ourselves filled with the light of Christ and with his Spirit. In order to be able to share effectively in bearing the Church's burdens we must first gain strength and wisdom. We must be educated in love. We must make a beginning of holiness.

No simple and efficacious formulas exist except in the Gospel, where they are not the words of man but the words of God. And, with all their transparent simplicity, the words of Christ, the words of salvation, remain as deeply mysterious as everything else which proceeds from God. Thus, while it is quite clear that we are called to "be perfect," and while we know that perfection consists in "keeping the commandments" (of Christ), above all his "new commandment to love one another as he has loved us," still each one has to work out his salvation in fear and trembling in the mystery and often bewildering confusion of his own individual life. In doing this, each one actually comes out with a new "way," a new "sanctity" which is all his own, because each one of us has a peculiar vocation to reproduce the likeness of Christ in a mode that is not quite the same as anybody else's, since no two of us are quite alike.

This "seeking" of the hidden and invisible God may seem to be very simple when it is reduced to clearly formulated laws and counsels of the spiritual life. It is not hard to imagine ourselves discovering certain things to be done which are good, and avoiding other things which are evil: doing good things generously, always of course "with the help of God's grace" and thus attaining to "divine union." With a more or less definite ideal in mind, we set out to conquer sanctity by forcing the realities of life to conform to our ideal. All that is needed, we believe, is generosity, complete fidelity to this ideal.

Unfortunately we forget that our ideal itself may be imperfect and misleading. Although our ideal is based on objective norms, we may interpret those norms in a very limited and subjective manner: we may distort them unconsciously to fit our own inordinate needs and expectations. These needs and expectations of ours, these demands we make on ourselves and on life—on God himself—may be much more absurd and illusory than we are capable of realizing. And therefore our whole idea of perfection, though it may be formulated in words that are theologically irreproachable, may be so utterly unreal in actual practice that we are reduced to helplessness and frustration. We may even "lose our vocation," not because we have no ideals, but because our ideals have no relation to reality.

The spiritual life is a kind of dialectic between ideals and reality. I say a dialectic, not a compromise. Ideals, which are generally based on universal ascetic norms "for everybody"—or at least for all those who are "seeking perfection"—cannot be realized in the same way in each individual. Each one becomes perfect, not by realizing one uniform standard of universal perfection in his own life, but by responding to the call and the love of God, addressed to him within the limitations and circumstances of his own peculiar vocation. In fact, our seeking of God is not all a matter of our finding him by means of certain ascetic techniques. It is rather a quieting and ordering of our whole life by self-denial, prayer, and good works, so that God himself, who seeks us more than we seek him, can "find us" and "take possession of us."

Let us recognize also that our concept of grace may be hazy and unreal. In fact, the more the notion of grace is treated by us in a semimaterialistic, objectified way, the more unreal it will be. In practice, we tend to think of grace as a kind of mysterious substance, a "thing," a commodity which is furnished us by God—something like fuel for a supernatural engine. We regard it as a kind of spiritual gasoline which we find necessary in order to make our journey to God.

Of course, grace is a great mystery, and can only be spoken of in analogies and metaphors which tend to be misleading. But certainly this metaphor is so misleading as to be altogether false. Grace is not "something with which" we perform good works and attain to God. It is not a "thing" or a "substance" entirely apart from God. It is God's very presence and action within us. Therefore, clearly it is not a commodity we "need to get" *from* him in order to go *to* him. For all practical purposes we might as well say that grace is the quality of our being that results from the sanctifying energy of God acting dynamically in our life. That is why in primitive Christian literature, and especially in the New Testament, we read not so much of receiving grace as of receiving the Holy Spirit—God himself.

We would do well to emphasize *uncreated* grace. The Holy Spirit present within us, the *dulcis hospes animae*, the "sweet guest dwelling in our soul." His very presence within us changes us from carnal to spiritual beings (Rom. 8:9), and it is a great pity that we are so little aware of this fact. If we realized the meaning and import of his intimate closeness to us, we would find in him constant joy, strength, and peace. We would be more attuned to that secret, inward "inclination of the Spirit which is life and peace" (Rom. 8:5). We would be better able to taste and enjoy the fruits of the Spirit (Gal. 5). We would have confidence in the hidden One who prays within us even when we ourselves are not able to pray well, who asks for us the things we do not know we need, and who seeks to give us joys we would not dare to seek for ourselves.

To "be perfect" then is not so much a matter of seeking God with ardor and generosity, as of being found, loved, and possessed by God, in such a way that his action in us makes us completely generous and helps us to transcend our limitations and react against our own weakness. We become saints not by violently overcoming our own weakness, but by letting the Lord give us the strength ahd purity of his Spirit in exchange for our weakness and misery. Let us not then complicate our lives and frustrate ourselves by fixing too much attention on ourselves, thereby forgetting the power of God and grieving the Holy Ghost.

Our spiritual attitude, our way of seeking peace and perfection, depends entirely on our concept of God. If we are able to believe he is truly our loving Father, if we can really accept the truth of his infinite and compassionate concern for us, if we believe that he loves us not because we are worthy but because we need his love, then we can advance with confidence. We will not be discouraged by our inevitable weaknesses and failures. We can do anything he asks of us. But if we believe he is a stern, cold lawgiver who has no real interest in us, who is merely a ruler, a lord, a judge and not a father, we will have great difficulty in living the Christian life. We must therefore begin by *believing* God is our Father: otherwise we cannot face the difficulties of the Christian way of perfection. Without faith, the "narrow way" is utterly impossible.

II. THE TESTING OF IDEALS

THE NEW LAW

In order to be perfect we must have concrete rational ideals and make efforts to live up to them. There must be some general norms and standards which apply to all, which serve as universal "rules" to be followed by each one in the living of his own life. Such rules must never be underestimated or neglected. If we here devote a few pages to reflection on these broad, general norms which are the basis of Christian spiritual doctrine, it is not because we are trying to map out a foolproof method for becoming holy. We are simply recalling to mind the Church's fundamental teaching on the way of Christian perfection.

The way of Christian perfection begins with a personal summons, addressed to the individual Christian by Christ the Lord, through the Holy Spirit. This summons is a call, a "vocation." Every Christian in one way or other receives this vocation from Christ—the call to follow him. Sometimes we imagine that vocation is the prerogative of priests and of religious. It is true that they receive a special call to perfection. They dedicate themselves to the quest for Christian perfection by the use of certain definite means. Yet every Christian is called to follow Christ, to imitate Christ as perfectly as the circumstances of his life permit, and thereby to become a saint.

Our reply to this call of Christ does not consist in saying many prayers, making many novenas, lighting vigil lights before the statues of the saints, or in eating fish on Friday. It does not merely consist in attendance at Mass, or the performance of certain acts of self-denial. All these things may be very good when seen in the full context of the Christian life. Taken out of this context they may be devoid of religious significance, mere empty gestures.

Our response to Christ means taking up our cross, and this in turn means shouldering our responsibility to seek and to do, in all things, the will of the Father. This was, in fact, the whole essence of Christ's own earthly life, and of his death and resurrection. All was done in obedience to the Father (Heb. 10:5–8; Lk. 2:49; Mt. 26:42; Jn. 5:30, etc.). So, too, Christ says to every Christian: "The kingdom of heaven will not give entrance to every man who calls me Master, Master; only to the man who does the will of my Father who is in heaven" (Mt. 7:21).

Hence our whole life should be centered on the will of the Father. This will is expressed clearly and obviously in the law given to us by God—summed up in the Ten Commandments and epitomized most perfectly in the one great commandment to love God with all our hearts and minds and strength, and to love our neighbor as ourselves.

But now that Christ has laid down his life and risen from the dead, to take possession of us by his Spirit, the Spirit himself, dwelling in us, should be to us a law. This interior law, the "New Law" which is purely a law of love, is summed up in the word "sonship." "Those who follow the leading of God's Spirit are all God's sons; the spirit you have now received is not, as of old, a spirit of slavery to govern you by fear; it is a spirit of adoption which makes us cry out Abba, Father" (Rom. 8:15).

The Holy Spirit does not abolish the Old Law, the *exterior* command: he makes that same law *interior* to ourselves, so that doing God's will becomes now no longer a work of fear but a work of spontaneous love.

Hence the Holy Spirit does not teach us to act contrary to the familiar dictates of law. On the contrary he leads us to the most perfect observance of Law, to the loving fulfillment of all our duties, in the family, in our work, in our chosen way of life, in our social relationships, in civic life, in our prayer, and in the intimate conversation with God in the depths of our souls.

The Holy Spirit teaches us not only actively to carry out the will of God as signified to us by precept, but also lovingly to accept the will of God in providential events beyond our own control.

In a word, the whole Christian life consists in seeking the will of God by loving faith and carrying out that blessed will by faithful love.

Perfection is therefore a question of *fidelity and love*— fidelity to duty first of all, then love of God's will in all its manifestations. Love implies *preference* and preference demands sacrifice. In practice, then, the preference of God's will means setting aside and sacrificing our own will. The more a Christian renounces his own will to do the will of God in loving submission and carefree abandonment, the more he will be united to Christ in the Spirit of divine sonship, the more truly will he show himself a son of the heavenly Father, and the closer he will come to Christian perfection.

WHAT IS THE WILL OF GOD?

Yet here another problem arises, and once again we ask ourselves if perhaps we do not need some kind of systematic, methodic way of knowing and doing the will of God. How am I going to be faithful to that mysterious and holy will? How do I know when a sacrifice is pleasing to the heavenly Father, and when it is only an illusion of my own will?

This is certainly not an easy matter. It cannot be left to subjective feeling or caprice. One might, for example, devise a fallacious and oversimplified method of discerning "the will of God." One might say: "normally my sinful will is opposed to God's will. Therefore to rectify this situation, I must always do what contradicts my spontaneous desires or my personal interests and then I will be sure of doing the will of God." But this starts out with a false premise, a kind of Manichaean assumption that I am necessarily inclined to evil at all times, that anything I spontaneously desire is bound, *a priori*, to be sinful.

Human nature is not evil. All pleasure is not wrong. All spontaneous desires are not selfish. The doctrine of original sin does not mean that human nature has been completely corrupted and that man's freedom is always inclined to sin. Man is neither a devil nor an angel. He is not a pure spirit, but a being of flesh and spirit, subject to error and malice, but basically inclined to seek truth and goodness. He is, indeed, a sinner: but his heart responds to love and grace. It also responds to the goodness and to the need of his fellow man.

The Christian way to discern the will of God is not

37

an abstract logical operation. Nor is it merely subjective. The Christian is a member of a living body, and his awareness of the will of God depends on his relatedness to the other members of the same body: because since we are all united as "members one of another," the living, salvific will of God is mysteriously communicated to us through one another. We all need one another, we all complete one another. God's will is found in this mutual interdependence. "A man's body is all one, though it has a number of different organs; and all this multitude of organs goes to make up one body; so it is with Christ. We too, all of us, have been baptized into a single body by the power of a single Spirit, Jews and Greeks, slaves and free men alike; we have all been given drink at a single source, the one Spirit. The body, after all, consists not of one organ but of many; if the foot should say, I am not the hand, and therefore I do not belong to the body, does it belong to the body any the less for that? If the ear should say, I am not the eye, and therefore I do not belong to the body, does it belong to the body any the less for that? Where would the power of hearing be, if the body were all eye? Or the power of smell, if the body were all ear? As it is, God has given each one of them its own position in the body, as he would. If the whole were one single organ, what would become of the body? Instead of that, we have a multitude of organs, and one body. The eye cannot say to the hand, I have no need of thee, or the head to the feet, I have no need of you" (1 Cor. 12:12–21).

The Christian "method" is then not a complex set of ritual observances and ascetic practices. It is above all an ethic of spontaneous charity, dictated by the objective relationship between the Christian and his brother. And every man is, to the Christian, in some sense a brother. Some are actually and visibly members of the Body of Christ. But all men are potentially members of that body, and who can say with certainty that the non-Catholic or the non-Christian is not in some hidden way justified by the indwelling Spirit of God and hence, though not visibly and obviously, a true brother "in Christ"?

The will of God is therefore manifested to the Christian above all in the commandment to love. Jesus Christ Our Lord said to his disciples in the most solemn of all his discourses that those who would love him would keep his commandment to love one another as he has loved us.

"All this I have told you, so that my joy may be yours, and the measure of your joy may be filled up. This is my commandment, that you should love one another, as I have loved you. This is the greatest love a man can show, that he should lay down his life for his friends; and you, if you do all that I command you, are my friends. I do not speak of you any more as my servants; a servant is one who does not understand what his master is about, whereas I have made known to you all that my Father has told me; and so I have called you my friends. It was not you that chose me, it was I that chose you. The task I have appointed you is to go out and bear fruit, fruit which will endure; so that every request you make of the Father in my name may be granted you. These are the directions I give you, that you should love one another" (Jn. 15:11-17).

This is the only ascetic "method" which Christ has given us in the Gospels: that all should show themselves his friends by being friends of one another, and by loving even their enemies (Mt. 5:43-48). If they should always behave in a spirit of sacrifice, patience, and meekness even toward the unjust and the violent, Christians are all the more strongly obligated to be charitable and kind to one another, never using vicious and insulting language toward one another (Mt. 5:20-26).

The Christian "method" of discovering the will of God is then to seek that holy and life-giving will in the mutual interrelationship of actual and potential members of the Mystical Body of Christ. The will of God is that all

39

should be saved. Hence it follows that God wills us all to cooperate with Jesus Christ and with one another to bring one another to salvation and holiness.

We are all bound to seek not only our own good, but the good of others. Divine providence brings us in contact, whether directly or indirectly, with those in whose lives we are to play a part as instruments of salvation. And the Holy Spirit also wills that we should receive from those to whom we give, and give to others from whom we receive. The whole Christian life is then an interrelationship between members of a body unified by supernatural charity, that is by the action of the Holy Spirit, making us all one in Christ. The will of God is above all that each one should cooperate as freely as possible with the Holy Spirit of love, the "bond of unity."

This unity is living and organic. The Church is more than an organization imposing on its members an external uniformity. It is a living organism which unites them by a life that is present and active in the depths of their own being. This life is Christian love. And it expresses itself in an almost infinite variety of ways, in the innumerable members of the Mystical Body. The will of God is then that each one should, according to his capacity, according to his function and position, devote himself to the service and salvation of all his brothers, especially of those who are closest to him in the order of charity. He must first love those nearest to him—parents, children, dependents, friends: but eventually his love must reach out to all men.

The norm by which we can evaluate and judge our sacrifices, then, is this precise order of charity. The sacrifice of our own will is necessary and pleasing to God whenever there is question of renouncing our individual, private good for a higher and more common good that will work both for our own salvation and the salvation of others. What matters then is not precisely what the sacrifice *costs us*, but what it will contribute to the good of others and of the Church. The norm of sacrifice is not the amount of pain it inflicts, but its power to break down walls of division, to heal wounds, to restore order and unity in the Body of Christ.

"Do to other men all that you would have them do to you; that is the law and the prophets. Make your way in by the narrow gate. It is a broad gate and a wide road that leads on to perdition, and those who go in that way are many indeed; but how small is the gate, how narrow the road that leads on to life, and how few there are that find it! Be on your guard against false prophets, men who come to you in sheep's clothing, but are ravenous wolves within. You will know them by the fruit they yield. Can grapes be plucked from briers, or figs from thistles? So, indeed, any sound tree will bear good fruit, while any tree that is withered will bear fruit that is worthless; that worthless fruit should come from a sound tree, or good fruit from a withered tree, is impossible. Any tree which does not bear good fruit is cut down, and thrown into the fire. I say therefore, it is by their fruit that you will know them. The kingdom of heaven will not give entrance to every man who calls me Master, Master; only to the man that does the will of my Father who is in heaven" (Mt. 7:12–21).

"If thou art bringing thy gift, then, before the altar, and rememberest there that thy brother has some ground of complaint against thee, leave thy gift lying there before the altar, and go home; be reconciled with thy brother first, and then come back to offer thy gift. If any man has a claim against thee, come to terms there and then, while thou art walking in the road with him; or else it may be that the claimant will hand thee over to the judge, and the judge to the officer, and so thou wilt be cast into prison. Believe me, thou shalt not be set at liberty until thou has paid the last farthing" (Mt. 5:23–26):

"Vain offerings, bring them no more; your very incense

is an abomination. Enough of new moons and sabbaths, of thronged assemblies where none but sinners meet! The new month begins, the feast day comes round, stale and wearisome, cloying the appetite. Hold out your hands as you will, you shall get no heed from me; add prayer to prayer, I will not listen; are not those hands stained with blood? Wash yourselves clean, spare me the sight of your busy wickedness, keep holiday from wrong-doing. Learn, rather, how to do good, setting your hearts on justice, righting the wrong, protecting the orphan, giving the widow redress; then come back, says the Lord, and make trial of me. Then, the scarlet dye of your guilt will show snow-white, the crimson stains will be like clean wool" (Is. 1:13-18).

The basic principle is then that each should recognize both his need of all the others and his obligation to serve all the others. The will of God will begin to come clear once this fundamental truth has been accepted and understood. But unless we recognize that we are members of one body and that we have vital obligations and responsibilities toward other members who live by the same life-principle, we will never understand the love of God.

LOVE AND OBEDIENCE

The priority of charity in the Christian moral life gives us the key to all the other obligations of a Christian. The Church must certainly have external laws and regulations. She must by all means make use of organizational discipline, ritual, a teaching authority. She must have a hierarchy. But when we forget the purpose of all these things, when we overlook their orientation to *union in charity*, we get a very distorted idea of the Church and of her life.

If we forget that the laws and organization of the Church are there only to preserve the inner life of charity, we will tend to make the observance of law an end in itself. Then the Christian life becomes externalized. He who has externally fulfilled the law may tend to be content with that, even if he is not closely united to his fellow Christian, and his fellow man, in sincere, humble, and selfless charity. He may eventually become so absorbed in the externals of law and of organization that he loses a real sense of the importance of charity in the Christian life. And this makes genuine holiness impossible, since holiness is the fullness of life, the abundance of charity and the radiation of the Holy Spirit hidden within us.

Christian charity obviously demands Christian obedience. The higher and more perfect union of wills in love will not be possible if the lower and more elementary union of wills in obedience is lacking. It is an error to appeal to love *against* obedience. But it is also an error to reduce all love in practice to obedience alone, as if the two were synonymous. Love is something much deeper than obedience, but unless obedience opens up those inner spiritual depths our love will remain superficial, a matter of sentiment and emotion, little more. Obedience can give love the strength to rise above the formalities of pure externalism. Without obedience our charity will be subjective and uncertain. We need objective norms by which to channel the strength of love in the direction willed by God in and for his Church. Obedience provides us with these objective standards.

It is very important to recall these simple basic principles that are so often taken for granted and, in practice, forgotten. Yet it is precisely this loss of true perspective that makes holiness seem like an impractical or indeed an impossible ideal for the Christian.

When we lose sight of the central element in Christian holiness, which is love, and when we forget that the way to fulfill the Christian commandment to love is not something remote and esoteric, but is on the contrary something immediately before us, then the Christian life becomes complicated and very confusing. It loses the simplicity and the unity which Christ gave it in his gospel, and it becomes a labyrinth of unrelated precepts, counsels, ascetic principles, moral cases, and even of legal and ritual technicalities. These things become difficult to understand in proportion as they lose their connection with charity which unites them all and gives them all an orientation to Christ.

Abashed by the complexities and difficulties of a disorganized and barely comprehensible spiritual life, we begin to believe that true Christian holiness is such an elaborate and technical affair that it can only be understood and practiced by experts.

Obviously it is good to have theological knowledge as well as experience in the ascetic life. It is good, too, to have enough learning to realize the true meaning of law and liturgical prescriptions in the Catholic life. A properly oriented study of these things tells us that, as, Adam of Perseigne, one of the Cistercian writers of the twelfth century said: "Law is simply love that binds and obliges" (Lex est amor qui ligat et obligat.).

It is possible however that the confusion and misunderstanding that arise, when one forgets the primacy of charity in Christian life, may lead to such a state of disillusionment that one gives up altogether trying to be holy, or even profoundly Christian. This involves a severe testing of ideals. It is a test in which one may easily fail. The answer is not just "effort" and "will power." On the contrary, intellectual and spiritual light may sometimes be the most necessary element in saving one's vocation to holiness and even one's Christian faith. Will power is ineffectual without truth. Love without truth is mere sentimentality.

ADULT CHRISTIANS

It can easily happen that a person loses his Christian faith as a result of *forcing himself* to try to accept a view of the Church, or of God, or of life in Christ, which is so distorted that it is practically false. Yet he may be under the impression that this view of the Church is the right one, since it appears to be the view actually held by most of the Christians with whom he associates. In such cases, the effort to cling to a deficient and imperfect concept of Christianity not only does no good, but actually contributes more quickly and effectively to loss of faith. What is necessary in such a situation is not *force*, not self-castigation and confused efforts to conform to second-rate Christians, so much as a clarification of the real issue and a restoration of true perspectives.

Our ideals must surely be tested in the most radical way. We cannot avoid this testing. Not only must we revise and renew our idea of holiness and of Christian maturity (not fearing to cast aside the illusions of our Christian childhood), but we may also have to confront in our lives inadequate ideas of God and the Church. Indeed, we may have to grapple with actual abuses in the life of Christians, in a so-called Christian society, and even in the Church herself.

Indeed, the concept of a "Christian society" is one that needs to be clarified today. Certainly the affluent, secularized society of modern Europe and America has ceased to be genuinely Christian. Yet in this society Christians tend to cling to vestiges of their own tradition which still survive, and because of these vestiges they believe that they are still living in a Christian world. Without a doubt the pragmatism and secularism of the nineteenth and twentieth centuries have entered deeply into the thought and spirit of the average Christian. On the other hand, the violent defensive reaction of the Church in the nineteenth century against the French Revolution and its consequences has left a spirit of rigidity and even a certain fear of new developments. This difficult situation results in many conflicts and apparent contradictions in Catholic life. There can be no doubt that the Church today is facing one of the greatest crises in her history. Obviously then there will be scandals and problems of conscience on every side.

It is normal and necessary for a mature Christian to have to confront, at some time or other, the inevitable shortcomings of Christians—of others as well as of himself. It is both dishonest and unfaithful for a Christian to imagine that the only way to preserve his faith in the Church is to convince himself that everything is always, in every way, at all times, ideal in her life and activity. History is there to prove the contrary. It is unfortunately true that Christians themselves, for one reason or another, may in the name of God himself and of his truth, cling to subtle forms of prejudice, inertia, and mental paralysis. Indeed there may even be serious moral disorders and injustices where holiness should prevail. Certainly the Church herself never teaches error, and never promotes injustice. But her faithful may in various ways make use of the Church's teaching and discipline to entrench themselves in a situation which seems favorable to themselves, and which in fact contains many elements of falsity, of dishonesty, and of injustice. Or they may simply train themselves to ignore the true import of the Church's teaching, and then fail in their obligation to uphold justice and truth, whether in the spiritual realm or in society itself.

The Christian must learn how to face these problems

with a sincere and humble concern for truth and for the glory of God's Church. He must learn to help correct these errors, without falling into an indiscreet or rebellious zeal. Arrogance is never a sign of grace. As St. Peter Damian said, to the monks of Vallombrosa who were infuriated against very real abuses in the Church of the eleventh century: "Let him who wants to be holy first of all be holy in himself before God, and let him have no arrogance toward his weaker brother" (*Opusculum*, 30). The same saint opposed the arbitrary and general infliction of very severe penalties on whole groups of Christians and he did not believe that religious reforms could be successfully carried out by force of arms.

In all things, the Christian spirit is a spirit of love, humility, and service, not a spirit of violence in defense of absolutism and power. Hence, though there are real abuses always present in any institution, even in the Church, they must be faced with honesty, humility, and love. They cannot be glossed over or ignored. Not everyone can "do something" about problems which are too vast for a single individual to understand. But all can use them to good purpose in their own interior lives, regarding them as opportunities to purify their faith, their spirit of obedience, and their supernatural love of the Church.

Some Christians are not even able to face this task directly: they can never fully admit it to themselves. But they cannot escape the anguish which wrings their heart. Perhaps they do not know the source of the anguish, but it is there. Others are able to admit to themselves that they see what they see: but it becomes a serious scandal to them. They rebel against the situation, they condemn the Church, and they even try to find the means to break away from it. They do not realize that they have now come close to the real meaning of their Christian vocation, and that they are now in a position to make the sacrifice that is demanded of adult Christian men and women: the realistic acceptance of imperfection and of deficiency in themselves, in others, and in their most cherished institutions.

They must face the truth of these imperfections, in order to see that the Church does not merely exist to do everything for them, to create a haven of peace and security for them, to sanctify them passively. On the contrary, it is now time for them to give to their community from their own heart's blood and to participate actively and generously in all its struggles. It is time to sacrifice themselves for others who may no longer seem to be very worthy. "I would remind you of this, he who sows sparingly will reap sparingly; he who sows freely will reap freely too. Each of you should carry out the purpose he has formed in his heart, not with any painful effort; it is the cheerful giver God loves. God has the power to supply you abundantly with every kind of blessing, so that, with all your needs well supplied at all times, you may have something to spare for every work of mercy" (2 Cor. 9:6–8).

It takes great heroism to devote one's life to others in a situation which is frustrating and unsatisfactory, and in which one's sacrifice may even be, in large measure, wasted. But here above all, faith in God is necessary. He sees our sacrifice, and he will make it fruitful, even though in our own eyes there is nothing apparent but futility and frustration. When we accept this grace, our eyes are opened to see the real, unsuspected good in others, and to be truly grateful for our Christian vocation.

REALISM IN THE SPIRITUAL LIFE

John Tauler says in one of his sermons that when God is seeking our soul he acts like the woman in the Gospel parable, who lost her groat and turned the whole house upside down until she had found it. This "upsetting" of our inner life is essential to spiritual growth, because without it we remain comfortably at rest in more or less illusory ideas of what spiritual perfection really is. In the doctrine of St. John of the Cross this is described as the "dark night" of passive purification that empties us of our too human concepts of God and of divine things, and leads us into the desert where we are nourished not by bread alone but by the means which can come only directly from him. Modern theologians have argued at some length about the necessity of passive mystical purification for fully mature Christian sanctity. We can here disregard the arguments on either side, since it is enough to say that true sanctity means the full expression of the cross of Christ in our lives, and this cross means the death of what is familiar and normal to us, the death of our everyday selves, in order that we may live on a new level. And yet, paradoxically, on this new level we recover our old, ordinary selves. It is the familiar self who dies and rises in Christ. The "new man" is totally transformed, and yet he remains the *same person*. He is spiritualized, indeed the Fathers would say he is "divinized" in Christ.

This should warn us that it is useless to cherish "ideals" which, as we imagine, will help us to escape from a self with which we are dissatisfied or disgusted. The way of perfection is not a way of escape. We can only become saints by facing ourselves, by assuming full responsibility for our lives just as they are, with all their handicaps and limitations, and submitting ourselves to the purifying and transforming action of the Saviour.

It is really tragic to observe the frustration and the ruin which overtake well-meaning but misguided young people who cannot grasp this elementary fact. For such, there is practically no question of a serious religious commitment. And yet they seem to be the ones who, in some way, are most hungry for perfection. The earnestness and intensity with which they seek to break out of the prison which they have become to themselves is so pathetic that it cannot help arousing compassion in all who try to help them. Sometimes, spiritual directors make the mistake of encouraging the illusory idealism which is the source of all the trouble, instead of trying to bring these poor sufferers to face reality.

There is no good in a morbid self-hatred which sometimes passes for humility. There is no hope in a spiritual ideal tainted with a Manichaean hatred of the body and of material things. An angelism which is nothing but a refinement of infantile self-love cannot lead either to spiritual liberty or to holiness.

And yet at the same time we must struggle to control our passions, we must seek to pacify our spirit in deep humility and abnegation, we must be able to say No firmly and definitely to our inordinate desires, and we must mortify even some of our legitimate cravings, for the sake of discipline.

The job of giving ourselves to God and renouncing the world is deeply serious, admitting of no compromise. It is not enough to meditate on a way of perfection that includes sacrifice, prayer, and renunciation of the world. We have to actually fast, pray, deny ourselves, and become interior men if we are ever going to hear the voice of God within us. It is not enough simply to make all perfection consist in active works, and to say that the observances and the duties imposed on us by obedience are by themselves sufficient to transform our whole lives in Christ. The man who simply "works for" God exteriorly may lack that interior love for him which is necessary for true perfection. Love seeks not only to serve him but to know him, to commune with him in prayer, to abandon itself to him in contemplation.

III. CHRIST, THE WAY

Perfection is not a moral embellishment which we acquire outside of Christ, in order to qualify for union with him. Perfection is the work of Christ himself living in us by faith. Perfection is the full life of charity perfected by the gifts of the Holy Ghost. In order that we may attain to Christian perfection, Jesus has left us his teachings, the sacraments of the Church, and all the counsels by which he shows us the way to live more perfectly in him and for him. For those with a special call to perfection, there is the religious state with its vows. Under the direction of the Church herself, we seek to correspond generously with the inspirations of the Holy Spirit. Inwardly guided by the Spirit of Christ, outwardly protected and formed by the visible Church with her hierarchy, her laws, teaching, sacraments, and liturgy, we grow together into "One Christ."

We must not regard the Church purely as an institution or an organization. She is certainly visible and clearly recognizable in her teachings, her government, and her worship. These are the external lineaments through which we may see the interior radiance of her soul. This soul is not merely human, it is divine. It is the Holy Spirit itself. The Church, like Christ, lives and acts in a manner at once human and divine. Certainly there is imperfection in the human members of Christ, but their imperfection is inseparably united to his perfection, sustained by his power, and purified by his holiness, as long as they remain in living union with him by faith and love. Through these members of his the Almighty Redeemer infallibly sanctifies, guides, and instructs us, and he uses us also to express his love for them. Hence the true nature of the Church is that of a body in which all the members "bear one another's burdens" and act as instruments of divine providence in regard to one another. Those are most sanctified who enter most fully into the life-giving Communion of Saints who dwell in Christ. Their joy is to taste the pure streams of that river of life whose waters gladden the whole City of God.

Our perfection is therefore not just an individual affair, it is also a question of growth in Christ, deepening of our contact with him in and through the Church, consequently a deepening of our participation in the life of the Church, the mystical Christ. This means, of course, a closer union with our brethren in Christ, a closer and more fruitful integration with them in the living, growing spiritual organism of the Mystical Body.

This does not mean that spiritual perfection is a matter of social conformism. The mere fact of becoming a well working cog in an efficient religious machine will never make anyone into a saint if he does not seek God interiorly in the sanctuary of his own soul. For example, the common life of religious, regulated by traditional observances and blessed by the authority of the Church, is obviously a most precious means of sanctification. It is, for the religious, one of the essentials of his state. But it is still only a framework. As such, it has its purpose. It must be used. But the scaffolding must not be mistaken for the actual building. The real building of the Church is a union of hearts in love, sacrifice, and self-transcendence. The strength of this building depends on the extent to which the Holy Spirit gains possession of each person's heart, not on the extent to which our exterior conduct is organized and disciplined by an expedient system. Human social life inevitably requires a certain order, and those who love their brother in Christ will generously sacrifice themselves to preserve this order. But the order is not an end in itself and mere orderliness is not yet sanctity.

Too often, people who take the spiritual life seriously may waste all their efforts on the scaffolding, making it more and more solid, permanent and secure, and paying no attention to the building itself. They do so out of a kind of unconscious fear of the real responsibilities of the Christian life, which are solitary and interior. These are difficult to express, even obliquely. They are almost impossible to communicate to anyone else. Hence one can never be "sure" whether he is right or wrong. One has very little evidence of progress or perfection in this interior sphere—while in the exterior, progress can be more easily measured and results can be seen. They can also be *shown* to others for their approval and admiration.

The most important, the most real, and lasting work of the Christian is accomplished in the depths of his own soul. It cannot be seen by anyone, even by himself. It is known only to God. This work is not so much a matter of fidelity to visible and general standards, as of *faith*: the interior, anguished, almost desperately solitary act by which we affirm our total subjection to God by grasping his word and his revelation of his will in the inmost depths of our being, as well as in obedience to the authority constituted by him.

The Credo which we triumphantly chant in the liturgy, in union with the whole Church, is real and valid only insofar as it expresses the inner self-commitment of each one to God's will, as manifested exteriorly through the Church and her hierarchy, and interiorly through the inspirations of divine grace.

Our faith is then a total surrender to Christ, which places all our hopes in him and in his Church, and expects all strength and sanctity from his merciful love.

SANCTITY IN CHRIST

From what has so far been said, it should be clear that Christian holiness is not a mere matter of ethical perfection. It includes every virtue, but is evidently more than all virtues together. Sanctity is not constituted only by good works or even by moral heroism, but first of all by ontological union with God "in Christ." Indeed, to understand the New Testament teaching on holiness of life we have to understand the meaning of this expression of St. Paul's. The moral teaching of the epistles always follows upon and elucidates a doctrinal exposition of the meaning of our "life in Christ." St. John, also, made it quite clear that all spiritual fruit in our life comes from union with Christ, integration in his Mystical Body as a branch is united with the vine and integrated in it (Jn. 15:1–11). This of course does not by any means reduce virtues and good works to insignificance: but these always remain secondary to our *new being*. According to the scholastic maxim, *actio sequitur esse*, action is in accordance with the being that acts. As the Lord himself said, you cannot gather figs from thistles. Hence we must first be transformed interiorly into new men, and then act according to the Spirit given to us by God, the Spirit of our new life, the Spirit of Christ. Our ontological holiness is our vital union with the Holy Spirit. Our striving to obey the Holy Spirit constitutes our moral goodness.

Hence what matters above all is not this or that observance, this or that set of ethical practices, but our renewal, our "new creation" in Christ (see Gal. 6:15). It is when we are united to Christ by "faith that works through charity" (Gal. 5:6) that we possess in ourselves the Holy Spirit who is the source of all virtuous action and of all love. The Christian life of virtue is not only a life in which we strive to unite ourselves to God by the practice of virtue. Rather it is also a life in which, drawn to union with God in Christ by the Holy Spirit, we strive to express our love and our new being by acts of virtue. Being united to Christ, we seek with all possible fervor to let him manifest *his* virtue and *his* sanctity in our lives. Our efforts should be directed to removing the obstacles of selfishness, disobedience, and all attachment to what is contrary to his love.

When the Church sings in the Gloria, *Tu solus sanctus* —"Thou, O Christ, alone art holy!"—we can interpret this to mean, surely, that all else that is holy is holy in and through him. It is through Christ that the sanctity of God is communicated and revealed to the world. If then we are to be holy, Christ must be holy in us. If we are to be "saints," he must be our sanctity. For, as St. Paul says: "To those who are called, Christ Jesus is the power of God and the wisdom of God. . . . Christ Jesus has become for us God-given wisdom and justice and sanctification and redemption; so that, just as it is written, 'let him who takes pride take pride in the Lord'" (1 Cor. 1:24, 30). But this all demands our own consent and our energetic cooperation with divine grace.

Jesus Christ, God and man, is the revelation of the hidden sanctity of the Father, the immortal and invisible King of Ages whom no eye can see, whom no intelligence can contemplate, except in the light which he himself communicates to whomever he wills. Hence, Christian "perfection" is not a mere ethical adventure or an achievement in which man can take glory. It is a gift of God, drawing the soul into the hidden abyss of the divine mystery, through the Son, by the action of the Holy Spirit. To be a Christian then is to be committed to a deeply mystical life, for Christianity is pre-eminently a mystical religion. This does not mean, of course, that every Christian is or should be a "mystic" in the technical modern sense of the word. But it does mean that every Christian lives, or should live, within the dimensions of a completely mystical revelation and communication of the divine being. Salvation, which is the goal of each individual Christian and of the Christian community as a whole, is participation in the life of God who draws us "out of darkness into his marvelous light" (1 Pt. 2:9). The Christian is one whose life and hope are centered in the mystery of Christ. In and through Christ, we become "partakers of the divine nature"—*divinae consortes naturae* (2 Pt. 1:4).

It is through Christ that the power of divine love and the energy of divine light find their way into our lives and transform them from one degree of "brightness" to another, by the action of the Holy Spirit. Here is the root and basis of the inner sanctity of the Christian. This light, this energy in our lives, is commonly called grace.

The more grace and love shine forth in the fraternal unity of those who have been brought together, by the Holy Spirit, in one Body, the more Christ is manifested in the world, the more the Father is glorified, and the closer we come to the final completion of God's work by the "recapitulation" of all things in Christ (Eph. 1:10).

GRACE AND THE SACRAMENTS

Our divine sonship is the likeness of the Word of God in us produced by his living presence in our souls, through the Holy Spirit. This is our "justice" in God's sight. It is the root of true love and of every other virtue. Finally it is the seed of eternal life: it is a divine inheritance which cannot be taken from us against our own will. It is an inexhaustible treasure, a fountain of living water "springing up unto life everlasting." The first epistle of St. Peter opens with a jubilant hymn in praise of this life of grace, freely given to us by the divine mercy, in Christ: the grace which leads to our salvation, if only we are faithful to the love of God that has been given to us when we were dead in our sins, raising us from death by the same power which raised Christ from the dead:

"Blessed be the God and Father of Our Lord Jesus Christ, who according to his great mercy has begotten us again, through the resurrection of Jesus Christ from the dead unto a living hope, unto an incorruptible inheritance—undefiled and unfading, reserved for you in heaven. By the power of God you are guarded through faith for salvation, which is to be revealed in the last time. Over this you rejoice; though now for a little while, if need be, you are made sorrowful by various trials, that the temper of your faith—more precious by far than gold which is tried by fire—may be found unto praise and glory and honor at the revelation of Jesus Christ. Him, though you have not seen, you love. In him, though you do not see him, yet believing, you exult with a joy unspeakable and triumphant; receiving as the final issue of your faith the salvation of your souls" (1 Pt. 1:3–9).

To say that the Christian religion is mystical is to say that it is also *sacramental*. The sacraments are "mysteries" in which God works, and our spirit works together with him under the impulsion of his divine love. We should not forget that the sacraments are mystical *signs* of a free spiritual work of divine love in our souls. The visible, external action by which a sacrament is conferred is not something which "causes" God to give grace though it causes us to receive grace. It is a sign that God is freely granting us his grace. The sign is necessary for us, but not for him. It awakens our hearts and our minds to respond to his actions. His grace could equally well be given *without* any external sign, but in that event most of us would be far less able to profit by the gift, to receive it efficaciously and correspond to it with the love of our hearts. We therefore need these holy signs as causes of grace in ourselves, but we do not, by them, exert a causal pressure on God. Quite the contrary!

If God has willed to communicate to us his ineffable light and share with us his life, he must himself determine the way in which this communication and sharing are to take place. He begins by addressing to man his *word*. When man hears and receives the word of God, obeys his summons and responds to his call, then he is brought to the font of baptism, or to the cleansing rivers of penance. He is nourished with the Blessed Eucharist in which the Body of the Lord is given to us to be our true spiritual food, the pledge of our eternal salvation and of our marriage with the Logos. Jesus wants us to "come to him" not only by faith, but also in sacramental union: for union with Christ in all the sacraments and particularly in the Blessed Eucharist not only signifies and symbolizes our complete mystical integration in him, but also produces that which it signifies. "He who eats my flesh and drinks my blood abides in me and I in him. As the living Father has sent me and as I live because of the father, so he who eats me, he also shall live because of me" (Jn. 6:57–58).

The most sanctifying action a Christian can perform is to receive Christ in the Eucharistic mystery, thus mystically participating in his death and resurrection, and becoming one with him in spirit and in truth. It is through faith and the sacraments of faith that we participate in the life of Christ. The Christian mystery is enacted and fulfilled among us by means of the sacramental worship of the Church. But in order to participate in that worship we must first become members of Christ by baptism.

By baptism, our souls are cleansed of sin and detached from selfish desires, liberated from the servitude of corruption to worship the living God as his sons. It is necessary that a man be baptized, if he is to enter into the mystery of Christ—the Kingdom of God. "Unless a man be born again of water and the Spirit, he cannot enter into the kingdom of God" (Jn. 3:5).

When we speak of this mystical way to God through the sacraments, we must be careful not to give the impression that sacramental mysticism is a kind of magic. This would be the case if the sacraments produced grace infallibly without any reference to the dispositions and correspondence of the one who receives them. It is true that the power of the sacraments, working *ex opere operato*, produces a salutary effect even when the worshiper is not able to elicit subjective sentiments of fervent devotion. In other words, the sacramental system is objective in its operation, but grace is not communicated to one who is not properly disposed. The sacraments produce no fruit where there is no love. When a catechumen is baptized by water, he is interiorly cleansed and transformed by the Holy Spirit; but this implies a choice and a self-commitment, it implies an acceptance of an obligation, and the determination to lead a Christian life. Baptism is not fruitful unless one means thereby to receive new life in Christ and to give himself forever to Christ. And this means renunciation of sin and dedication to a life of charity. It means living up to the dignity of our new being in Christ. It means living as sons of God.

"As many as received him he gave them power to be made the sons of God, to them that believe in his name, who are born not of blood, nor of the will of the flesh, nor of the will of man, but of God" (Jn. 1:12, 13).

"God is light, and in him there is no darkness. If we say we have fellowship with him and walk in darkness, we lie and are not practicing the truth. But if we walk in the light, as he also is in the light, we have fellowship with one another, and the blood of Jesus Christ, his Son, cleanses us from all sin. . . . My dear children, these things I write to you in order that you may not sin. But if anyone sin, we have an advocate with the Father, Jesus Christ, the just; and he is a propitiation for our sins, not for ours only but for those of the whole world.

"And by this we can be sure we know him, if we keep his commandments. He who says that he knows him and does not keep his commandments, is a liar and the truth is not in him. But he who keeps his word, in him the love of God is perfected; and by this we know that we are in him. He who says that he abides in him, ought himself to walk just as he walked" (1 Jn. 1:5–7, 2:1–6).

The sanctity of Christian life is based not on love of an abstract law but on love of the living God, a divine person, Jesus Christ, the Incarnate Word of God, who has redeemed us and delivered us from the darkness of sin. And it is based also on the love of our brothers in Christ. Hence our moral life is not legalistic, not a mere matter of fidelity to duty. It is above all a matter of personal gratitude, of love, and of praise. It is a "eucharistic" morality, a code of love based on communal thanksgiving and appreciation of our new life in Christ. This appreciation implies a deep understanding of the divine mercy which has brought us to share together in the death and resurrection of Christ. It implies a spiritual awareness of the fact that our Christian life is in fact the life of the risen Christ active and fruitful within all of us at every moment. Our morality is then centered on love and on *praise*, on the desire to see the risen Lord and Saviour fully glorified in our lives and in our community.

We must realize that our acts of virtue and our good works are not done simply in order to satisfy the cold obligation of an impersonal law. They are a personal response of love to the desire of a human Heart filled with divine love for us. The Sacred Heart of the risen Saviour communicates to our own inmost being every least impulse of grace and charity by which he shares with us his divine life. Our response is then an answer to the warm and sensitive promptings of the Lord's personal love for us. This realization not only diverts our attention from ourselves to him, but it also arouses a deeper and more vital hope, and awakens in our heart a more fruitful and dynamic faith. It fills our Christian life with the inexpressible warmth of gratitude and with a transcendent awareness of what it means to be sons of God because the only-begotten Son of the Father has loved us even to the point of dying for us on the cross, that we may be united in his love.

Not only are we grateful for our deliverance from sin by Christ, but Paul also makes clear that our "eucharistic" morality of grateful love is nourished by a sense of deliverance from a seemingly inescapable conflict. While we were under the law, says the Apostle (Rom. 7:13–25), we realized only our incapacity to be holy and to satisfy its stern demands. But now, by the grace of the loving Saviour, we have been able to keep the law and go much further than the law prescribed, in the perfection of love, because Christ himself has come, has put sin to death in our hearts, and has brought forth charity within us.

It is only because we have Christ dwelling in us that we can now satisfy the demands of the law. But the way of our doing so is to fix our eyes not on the law, but on Christ. We must occupy our hearts not with the thought of arduous and cold obligations which we do not fully understand, but with the presence and love of the Holy Spirit who enkindles in us the love of good and shows us how to "do all things in the name of Jesus Christ." The Christian way of perfection is then in every sense a way of love, of gratitude, of trust in God. Nowhere do we depend on our own strength or our own light: our eyes are fixed on Christ who gives all light and strength through his body, the Church. Our hearts are attentive to his Holy Spirit dwelling in our hearts and in the Church. The Lord himself then gives us power and guides us in a way that we do not understand, in proportion as we are united to him through charity, as living and active members of his body, the Church.

Our only concern is to be constantly and generously loyal to his Will as manifested especially in the community of the faithful. Our whole morality is to trust him even when we seem to be walking in the darkness of death, knowing that he is life and truth, and that where Jesus leads us there can be no error. The whole Christian way is summed up by St. Paul:

"There is therefore now no condemnation for those who are in Christ Jesus, who do not walk according to the flesh. For the law of the Spirit of the life in Christ Jesus has delivered me from the law of sin and of death. For what was impossible to the Law in that it was weak because of the flesh, God has made good" (Rom. 8:1-3).

FLESH AND SPIRIT

The only thing the Apostle asks us is to "walk" (that is, to live) not according to "the flesh" but according to the "spirit." This means several things. The flesh is the generic term not for bodily life (since the body along with the soul is sanctified by the Holy Spirit) but for *mundane* life. The "flesh" includes not only sensuality and licentiousness, but even worldly conformism, and actions based on human respect or social preoccupation.

We obey the "flesh" when we follow the norms of prejudice, complacency, bigotry, group-pride, superstition, ambition, or greed. Hence even an apparent holiness, based not on sincerity of heart but on hypocritical display, is of the "flesh." Whatever may be the "inclination of the flesh," even when it seems to point to heroic and dazzling actions admired by men, it is always death in the sight of God. It is not directed to him but to men around us. It does not seek his glory, but our own satisfaction. The spirit, on the other hand, leads us in the ways of life and peace.

The laws of the spirit are laws of humility and love. The spirit speaks to us from a deep inner sanctuary of the soul which is inaccessible to the flesh. For the "flesh" is our external self, our false self. The "spirit" is our real self, our inmost being united to God in Christ. In this hidden sanctuary of our being the voice of our conscience is at the same time our own inner voice and the voice of the Holy Spirit. For when one becomes "spirit" in Christ, he is no longer himself alone. It is not only he who lives, but

Christ lives in him, and the Holy Spirit guides and rules his life. Christian virtue is rooted in this inner unity in which our own self is one with Christ in the Spirit, our thoughts are able to be those of Christ and our desires to be his desires.

Our whole Christian life is then a life of union with the Holy Spirit and fidelity to the divine will in the depths of our being. Therefore it is a life of truth, of utter spiritual sincerity, and by that token it implies heroic humility. For truth, like charity, must begin at home. We must not only see ourselves as we are, in all our nothingness and insignificance; we must not only learn to love and appreciate our own emptiness, but we must accept completely the reality of our life as it is, because it is the very reality which Christ wills to take to himself, which he transforms and sanctifies in his own image and likeness.

If we are able to understand the presence of evil within us, we will be calm and objective enough to deal with it patiently, trusting in the grace of Christ. This is what is meant by following the Holy Spirit, resisting the flesh, persevering in our good desires, denying the claims of our false exterior self, and thus giving the depths of our heart to the transforming action of Christ:

"You are not carnal but spiritual if indeed the Spirit of God dwells in you. . . . If Christ is in you, the body, it is true, is dead by reason of sin, but the spirit is life by reason of justification. But if the Spirit of him who raised Jesus Christ from the dead dwells in you, then he who raised Christ Jesus from the dead will also bring to life your mortal bodies because of his Spirit who dwells in you" (Rom. 8:9–11).

Hence, when we are united to Christ by baptism, faith, and love, there may be many evil tendencies still at work in our body and psyche—seeds and roots of "death" remaining from our past life: but the Holy Spirit gives us grace to resist their growth, and our will to love and serve God in spite of these tendencies ratifies his life-giving action. Thus what he "sees" in us is not so much the evil that was ours but the good that is his.

IV. THE LIFE OF FAITH

FAITH IN GOD

The difference between "flesh" and "spirit" is therefore not a difference between sensuality and spirituality, between passion and detachment. A person can be detached and spiritual in a rational, idealistic kind of way, and still be "in the flesh" according to the New Testament (1 Cor. 3:1–4; Jas. 3:13–18). What distinguishes flesh from spirit is the virtue of *faith,* which gives us life "in the Spirit" and "in Christ." That is the meaning of the scriptural phrase: "the just man lives by faith." Justice here means holiness springing from union with God and expressed in all the virtues proper to a son of God (Gal. 5:6).

By faith Christ becomes the "power of God" in our lives. Only by faith can we truly accept Christ and his Church as our salvation. Without faith, one is a Christian in name only. One belongs to the Church, not as to the body of Christ but as to a social institution, a religious organization, and one conforms to the generally accepted norms of Christian behavior not out of love for God, not with any understanding of their inner meaning, but merely in order to live up to the minimum standard of good conduct which will guarantee acceptance by the group. Christ made it clear that there was a direct opposition between faith and human respect: "How can you believe who receive glory from one another, and do not seek the glory which is from the only God?" (Jn. 5:44).

If faith is so important, what is its real nature? Is it merely the intellectual acceptance of a few selected dogmas proposed to our belief by the authority of the Church? It is more. Naturally, faith implies the acceptance of dogmatic truth, but if it is only this, it does not go far enough. Merely to *submit*, even to submit one's judgment, is not yet the whole of faith. It is only one aspect of faith. In the last five centuries, due to the confusion of doctrines and the wrangling of sects, the authoritative definition of dogmatic truth has come to have a very great place in Catholic life. But this extraordinary emphasis must not give us a wrong perspective. Faith is not merely the acquiescence of the mind in certain *truths*, it is the gift of our whole being to *Truth itself*, to the Word of God.

THE EXISTENCE OF GOD

At the present day, when the existence of God has been denied or at least called into doubt by all the characteristically modern modes of thought, the problem of faith reduces itself, in many cases, to a problem of God's existence. This is certainly fundamental: "Without faith it is impossible to please God. For he who comes to God must believe that God exists and is a rewarder to those that seek him" (Heb. 11:6). A life of faith is certainly irrational unless it presupposes the reality of a God in whom to believe. And faith should be intelligent. It does not draw its light from reason and from intelligence—it is on the contrary a spiritual light for the intellect, coming from beyond the sphere of our own limited understanding. It is not a flat contradiction of reason, but transcends reason in a way that is still reasonable, hence St. Anselm's saying: *credo ut intelligam*, "I believe in order to understand." This is a more Christian, as well as a more human statement than Tertullian's *credo quia impossible* (I believe this because it is impossible) though the latter paradox is rhetorically significant as an expression of the mystery implicit in the Christian life.

The question of God's existence is obviously open to rational investigation, and it can be demonstrated scientifically. But the trouble is that scientific demonstration cannot convince when its terms are not accepted or understood. Those for whom the crisis of faith centers upon the acceptance of God's existence are therefore often caught in a philosophical blind alley and their religious problem loses all coherence as long as they cannot liquidate more primitive difficulties in the realm of semantics. And these difficulties become harder and harder to handle. The average modern man is therefore in a position where philosophic argument about the existence of God can become, in practice, almost completely irrelevant. To engage in an elaborate discussion of the point helps neither faith nor reason but only tends to obscure both and to reduce honest minds to a state of permanent frustration and invincible doubt.

This is all the more pitiful because we all, by our very nature as intelligent beings, tend to have a simple and natural awareness of the reality of God without which the mere question of his existence could not even arise in our minds (see Rom. 1:20). As soon as we become fully aware of our own existence, as soon as we grasp the reality of the world around us and of contingent being, we find ourselves face to face with the question of a Pure and Absolute Being, necessarily implied by the presence of our own relative and contingent existence. This primal intuition, which is of course not a "proof" of anything but merely a datum of human experience, can become the starting point for all kinds of good and bad philosophical reasoning. But it can very well awaken the intelligence and lead it on to an act of faith. It even constitutes a kind of permanent invitation to faith, and unless we go *against* this natural and thoroughly reasonable intuition and resist it with conscious argument, denying and reinterpreting it from the point of view of acquired notions—and perhaps prejudices—we may quite spontaneously find ourselves on the way to faith.

HUMAN FAITHS

The tendency of our modern society and of all its thought and culture is to deny and to deride this simple, natural awareness, and to make man from the very beginning both afraid of faith and ashamed of it. The first step to living faith is then, as it has always been one way or another, a denial and a rejection of the standards of thought complacently accepted by rationalistic doubt. And in actual practice what this usually amounts to is not the rejection of "reason" and the acceptance of "faith" but rather a choice between two faiths. One, a human, limited, external faith in human society with all its inert patrimony of assumptions and prejudices, a faith based on fear of solitude and on the need to "belong" to the group and to accept its standards with passive acquiescence. Or, in the second place, a faith in what we do not "see," a faith in the transcendent and invisible God, a faith that goes beyond all proofs, a faith that demands an interior revolution of one's whole self and a reorientation of one's existence *in a contrary sense* to the orientation taken by mundane prejudice. Such faith as this is a complete acceptance not only of the existence of God as a convenient hypothesis which makes the cosmos seem intelligible, but as the center and meaning of all existence, and more particularly of our own life.

In the days when western society was Christian there was necessarily a kind of ambiguity about a faith which was "given" along with all other social values. In such a situation, faith could easily be corrupted by prejudice, and could be a matter of superstitious belief in one's group rather than a true belief in God and a genuine adherence to the Mystical Body of Christ. Even today, when so many people instinctively grope for a kind of human security in "faith," it can happen that they are only partly seeking God. That is the danger of a "faith" that is too intimately connected with the idea of "peace" and psychological comfort. When a man is too eager to set his subjective anxieties at rest, he is in danger of selling out to embrace an unreal faith which will bring him, apparently without too much cost, the semblance of peace. The cost may not appear to be much: but if it is the renunciation of responsibility for one's soul, then it is great beyond measure.

NEW TESTAMENT FAITH

Here is the meaning of faith in the New Testament, and in the early history of the Church: the willingness to sacrifice every other value rather than the basic value of truth and life in Christ. Christian faith in the full sense of the word, is not just the acceptance of "truths about" Christ. It is not just acquiescence in the story of Christ with its moral and spiritual implications. It is not merely the decision to put into practice, to some extent at least, the teachings of Christ. All these forms of acceptance are compatible with an acquiescence in what is "not Christ." It is quite possible to "believe in Christ," in the sense of mentally accepting the truth that he lived on earth, died, and rose from the dead, and yet still live "in the flesh," according to the standards of a greedy, violent, unjust and corrupt society, without noticing any real contradiction in one's life.

But the real meaning of faith is *the rejection of everything that is not Christ in order that all life, all truth, all hope, all reality may be sought and found "in Christ."*

This of course must not be interpreted as a rejection of the material universe and of all of God's creation, for these too come from Christ, subsist in Christ, and have no other reason for existence than to serve the purposes of his mercy, truth, and love, thereby manifesting the glory of the Father. To reject the "world" is not to reject people, society, the creatures of God or the works of man, but to reject the perverted standards which make men misuse and spoil a good creation, ruining their own lives into the bargain:

"The things that were gain to me, these for the sake of Christ I have counted loss. Nay more I count everything as loss because of the excelling knowledge of Jesus Christ my Lord. For his sake I have suffered the loss of all things and I count them as dung that I may gain Christ and be found in him, not having a justice of my own, which is from the Law, but that which is from faith in Christ, the justice from God, based upon faith; so that I may know him and the power of his resurrection and the fellowship of his sufferings; become like to him in death in the hope that somehow I may attain to the resurrection from the dead" (Phil. 3:7–11).

This characteristic passage from St. Paul shows how sweeping is the New Testament concept of faith. To Christian faith, Christ is everything, and all that is not from Christ or in Christ is nothing: it is less than nothing, it is "dung." Such strong expressions have come to seem forbidding to the modern believer. They are not often used in sermons and pious writings, because they give the impression of being "extreme." And yet the Christian faith is itself "extreme," or at least absolute. Once it has "found" Christ, it sees the obligation to break completely with everything that is contrary to him, no matter how much this break may cost. It sees the obligation of unswerving fidelity to his love, no matter how difficult that fidelity may sometimes appear to be. Finally, it sees the need to rely completely on him in perfect trust, abandoning our whole life into his hands and letting him take care of us without our being able to see how he intends to do so. This is the genuine dimension of Christian faith.

Such faith is not only a subjective, psychological reaction: it is a dynamic and supernatural power in man's life. It is a "new creation," an act of the divine omnipotence, revolutionizing man's spiritual and bodily life in its inmost depths. That is why the synoptic Gospels echo with the words of Jesus Christ to those he has healed: "Thy faith hath made thee whole!"

In every case this faith is simply a total, unswerving acceptance of the person of Christ as a source of salvific power and of new life.

The faith by which we are united to Christ and receive supernatural life by the Gift of his Spirit, is not mere emotional or affective self-commitment. It is not a matter of blind will. Christ is not only our life, he is also our way and our truth (Jn. 14:6). Faith is an intellectual light by which we "know" the Father in the Incarnate Word (Jn. 14:7-14). Yet faith is at the same time a mysterious and obscure knowledge. It knows, as the medieval mystics said, by "unknowing." To believe is to know without seeing, to know without intrinsic evidence (2 Cor. 5:7). Or rather, while faith truly "sees," it sees *per speculum, in aenigmate* (1 Cor. 13:12), in a manner that is dark, mysterious, beyond explanation. The "vision" or intellectual illumination of faith is produced not by the natural activity of our intelligence working on sensible evidence, but by a direct supernatural action of the Spirit of God. Hence, though it is for that very reason beyond the normal grasp of the unaided intelligence, it offers a greater certitude than natural scientific knowledge. But this greater certitude, though it remains a matter of personal conviction, is not susceptible of rational proof to anyone who does not himself accept the premises of faith. "No man can come to me," said Jesus Christ, "unless he be drawn by the Father who sent me" (Jn. 6:44; cf. 6:65).

Faith is therefore a gratuitous gift of God, given according to God's good pleasure, refused by him to those who are obstinate in clinging to human prejudice and to the mythology of racial, national, or class pride. It is given to those who are disposed to accept the gift in simplicity and humility of heart, trusting not in the authority of political power or human prestige, but in the word of God speaking in his Church (Mt. 11:25-27).

Consequently it is necessary to dispose our hearts for faith in various ways, above all by inquiry, by reading, and by prayer. If we want to know what faith is, and what Christians believe, we must inquire of the Church. If we want to know what God has revealed to the believer, we must read the Scriptures, we must study those who have explained the Scriptures, and we must acquaint ourselves with the basic truths of philosophy and theology. But since faith is a gift, prayer is perhaps the most important of all the ways of seeking it from God.

After all, it is not always easy to find a Christian capable of explaining his faith, and even the clergy may not be able to translate technical knowledge into terms that everyone can grasp. The Bible, too, is not always easy to understand. Subjective interpretation of Scripture may lead to disastrous error. As for theology and philosophy: where will a man without religious education begin to find out about them? Prayer is then the first and most important step. All through the life of faith one must resort constantly to prayer, because faith is not simply a gift which we receive once for all in our first act of belief. Every new development of faith, every new increment of supernatural light, even though we may be earnestly working to acquire it, remains a pure gift of God.

Prayer is therefore the very heart of the life of faith.

When we read in the New Testament of faith "moving mountains" we must not interpret the symbolic language in an exclusively literal sense, as if it meant that prayer were a wonderful means of accomplishing physically difficult or impossible tasks. This is the kind of inanity that atheists come up with, after they have moved a hill with a bulldozer, or after a Russian astronaut has returned to earth without having seen angels. Faith does indeed deal with impossibilities: but it is not intended as a substitute for mere physical power, or medicine, or study, or human investigation.

When Christ taught his hearers that they must have faith, he did not intend that they merely should use it to change the landscape. He was telling men their faith should be of a kind that was not daunted by any obstacle or any apparent impossibility. The lesson was directed to the qualities of faith, not to the nature of the task to be done. The task did not matter, because *anything* that was necessary for salvation would be granted by God in answer to prayer.

The chief meaning of the New Testament teaching on prayer is then that the kingdom of heaven is open to those who beg, by prayer, to enter it. That supernatural aid will never be refused anyone who needs it and seeks it in the name of Christ (Jn. 16:23). Faith will be granted to those who are able to pray for it. The light of divine truth is never refused to the humble. But prayer must be persevering and insistent. It must not be divided by doubt and weakened by hesitation.

"Is there one of you who still lacks wisdom? God gives to all, freely and ungrudgingly; so let him ask God for it, and the gift will come. (Only it must be in faith that he asks, he must not hesitate; one who hesitates is like a wave out at sea, driven to and fro by the wind; such a man must not hope to win any gift from the Lord. No, a man who is in two minds will find no rest wherever he goes)" (Jas. 1:5-8).

Yet the question arises: is modern man, confused and exhausted by a multitude of words, opinions, doctrines and slogans, *psychologically capable* of the clarity and confidence necessary for valid prayer? Is he not so frustrated and deafened by conflicting propagandas that he has lost his capacity for deep and simple trust?

It is true that man's spirit has been degraded and debauched by the cynical abuse of means of communication. He has been reduced to the condition of a machine responding automatically to words that are fed to him.

Such a machine is not really capable of divine faith without a process of radical healing and restoration. The task of Christian renewal in society is therefore vital if men are going to recover their capacity to believe.

V. GROWTH IN CHRIST

CHARITY

Faith is the beginning of a new life. Life means growth—and development *toward a final complete maturity and perfection. What is this finished perfection for the Christian? The full manifestation of Christ in our lives.* "When Christ shall appear, who is your life, then you also shall appear with him in glory" (Col. 3:4). This is true Christian perfection!

What does this mean? It means the full revelation in us of the great mystery of God's love for the world in his plan to "re-establish all things in Christ" (Eph. 1:9-10). God's mercy must be revealed in us. Christ must shine forth with all his glory in us, his members. It must become fully evident that his charity has made us truly one in him.

"That they may all be one as thou Father in me and I in thee, that they may be one in us; that the world may believe that thou hast sent me" (Jn. 17:21). (Jesus had just said before this, "For them do I sanctify myself that they also may be sanctified in truth"; and he has prayed: "sanctify them in truth—thy word is truth"—Jn. 17:17, 19.)

Hence we see that personal faith and fidelity to Christ are not enough to make us perfect Christians. We do not go by ourselves to him, as isolated individuals. We go to him as members of his Mystical Body. It can be said that our holiness is proportioned to our capacity to serve as instruments of his love in establishing his kingdom and building up his Mystical Body. The more fruitful and healthy are our lives as members of Christ, the more we are able to communicate the Christ-life to others, in and through the Holy Spirit. The more we are able to give to them, the more we receive from Christ. All the secret influx of mystical life into our souls is intended not only for ourselves but for others. These who receive the most are those who have the most to give, and if they have more to give it is perhaps because more has been forgiven them (Lk. 7:47-48). They have a greater capacity to love Christ in their brother because they have a deeper and more intimate experience of their own sorrow and of his mercy. Suffering and spiritual poverty have taught them compassion and made them spiritually rich, for it is the merciful who are rich in mercy.

It is also the merciful who are rich in truth. Unless we learn the meaning of mercy by exercising it toward others, we never have any real knowledge of what it means to love Christ. Not because our mercy to others teaches us to love Christ, directly, but rather because Christ's love in our own lives acts dynamically to reach others *through us*, thereby revealing him to us in our own souls.

Without love and compassion for others, our own apparent "love" for Christ is a fiction:

"He who says he is in the light and hates his brother, is in the darkness still. He who loves his brother abides in the light, and for him there is no stumbling. But he who hates his brother is in the darkness, and he does not know whither he goes; because the darkness has blinded his eyes . . . In this we have come to know his love, that he laid down his life for us; and we likewise ought to lay down our lives for the brethren. He who has the goods of this world and sees his brother in need and closes his heart to him, how does the love of God abide in him? My dear children, let us not love in word, neither with the tongue, but in deed and truth" (1 Jn. 2:9-11; 3:16-18).

SOCIAL PERSPECTIVES OF CHARITY

Too often Christian charity is understood in an entirely superficial way, as though it were no more than gentleness, kindness, and affability. It certainly includes all these things, but it goes far beyond them. When charity is regarded as merely "being nice to" other people, this is generally because our outlook is narrow and takes in only our immediate neighbors, who share the same advantages and comforts as we. This conception tacitly excludes those who most need our love—those who are unfortunate, who suffer, who are poor, destitute, or who have nothing in this world and who therefore have a claim upon everyone else who has more than he himself strictly needs.

There is no charity without justice. Too often we think of charity as a kind of moral luxury, as something which we choose to practice, and which gives us merit in God's sight, at the same time satisfying a certain interior need to "do good." Such charity is immature and even in some cases completely unreal. True charity is love, and love implies deep concern for the needs of another. It is not a matter of moral self-indulgence, but of strict obligation. I am obliged by the law of Christ and of the Spirit to be concerned with my brother's need, above all with his greatest need, the need for love. How many terrible problems in relations between classes, nations, and races in the modern world arise from the sad deficiency of love! Worst of all, this deficiency has manifested itself very clearly among those who claim to be Christians! Indeed

Christianity has repeatedly been called upon to justify injustice and hate!

Christ himself, in the Gospel, describes the Last Judgment in terms that make charity the chief criterion of salvation. Those who have fed the hungry and given drink to the thirsty, given shelter to the stranger, visited the sick and the prisoner, are taken into the kingdom: for they did all these things to Christ himself. Those on the other hand who have failed to give bread to the hungry, drink to the thirsty, and all the rest, have failed to do these things to Christ: "As long as you did not do it for one of these least ones, you did not do it for me" (Mt. 25:31-46).

From this text and from one in the first epistle of St. John just quoted, we see that Christian charity is meaningless without concrete and exterior acts of love. The Christian is not worthy of his name unless he gives from his possessions, his time, or at least his concern in order to help those less fortunate than himself. The sacrifice must be real, not just a gesture of lordly paternalism which inflates his own ego while patronizing "the poor." The sharing of material goods must also be a sharing of the heart, a recognition of common misery and poverty and of brotherhood in Christ. Such charity is impossible without an interior poverty of spirit which identifies us with the unfortunate, the underprivileged, the dispossessed. In some cases this can and should go to the extent of leaving all that we have in order to share the lot of the unfortunate.

Moreover, a shortsighted and perverse notion of charity leads Christians simply to perform token acts of mercy, merely symbolic acts expressing good will. This kind of charity has no real effect in helping the poor: all it does is tacitly to condone social injustice and to help to keep conditions as they are—to help to keep people poor. In our day, the problem of poverty and suffering has become everybody's concern. It is no longer possible to close our eyes to the misery that exists everywhere in the world, even in the richest nations. A Christian has to face the fact that this unutterable disgrace is by no means "the will of God," but the effect of incompetence, injustice, and the economic and social confusion of our rapidly developing world. It is not enough for us to ignore such things on the ground that we are helpless, and can do nothing constructive about the situation. It is a duty of charity and of justice for every Christian to take an active concern in trying to improve man's condition in the world. At the very least, this obligation consists in becoming aware of the situation and forming one's own conscience in regard to the problems it offers. One is not expected to solve all the problems of the world; but one should know when one can do something to help alleviate suffering and poverty, and realize when one is implicitly cooperating in evils which prolong or intensify suffering and poverty. In other words, Christian charity is no longer real unless it is accompanied by a concern with social justice.

Of what use is it to hold seminars on the doctrine of the Mystical Body and on sacred liturgy, if one is completely unconcerned with the suffering, destitution, sickness, and untimely death of millions of potential members of Christ? We may imagine that all this poverty and suffering is far removed from our own country: but if we knew and understood our obligations toward Africa, South America, and Asia we would not be so complacent. However, we do not have to look beyond our own borders to find plenty of human misery in the slums of our big cities, and in less privileged rural areas. What are we doing about it?

It is not enough to reach into our pocket and hand over a few dollars. We must give not only our possessions but *ourselves* to our brother. Until we regain this deep sense of charity, we cannot understand the full depths of Christian perfection.

The epistle of St. James tells us that a Christian should not respect the rich man and despise the poor, but should on the contrary identify himself with the poor man and be poor himself, as Christ was poor:

"For if a man in fine apparel, having a gold ring, enters your assembly, and a poor man in mean attire enters also, and you pay attention to him who is clothed in fine apparel and say, 'Sit thou here in this good place'; but you say to the poor man, 'Stand thou there,' or, 'Sit by my footstool'; are you not making distinctions among yourselves and do you not become judges with evil thoughts? Listen my beloved brethren! Has not God chosen the poor of this world to be rich in faith and heirs of the kingdom which God has promised to those who love him? But you have dishonored the poor man. Do not the rich use their power to oppress you, and do they not drag you before judgment-seats? Do they not blaspheme the good name by which you are called?" (Jas. 2:2–7).

Further on in the same epistle, St. James speaks frankly to the unjust rich who have defrauded the poor of their wages:

"Your riches have rotted and your garments have become moth-eaten. Your gold and silver have rusted; and their rust will be a witness against you, and will devour your flesh as fire does. You have laid up treasure in the last days. Behold the wages of the laborers who reaped your fields which have been kept back by you unjustly, cry out; and their cry has entered into the ears of the Lord of Hosts. You have feasted upon earth and you have nourished your hearts on dissipation in the day of slaughter. You have condemned and put to death the just and he did not resist you" (Jas. 5:2–5).

To be one in Christ, we must all love one another as our own selves. To love another as oneself means to treat him as oneself, to desire for him everything that one desires for oneself. This desire has no meaning unless one is willing to take definite steps to help someone else. The parable of the Good Samaritan is often told in the pulpit: it may mean more than we think. It was the good Jews, the priest and the levite, who left the wounded man in the ditch. Only the stranger and the outcast condescended to help him. Who are we? Priests, levites, or Samaritans?

WORK AND HOLINESS

We have seen that Christian holiness can no longer be considered a matter purely of individual and isolated acts of virtue. It must also be seen as part of a great collaborative effort for spiritual and cultural renewal in society, to produce conditions in which all men can work and enjoy the just fruits of their labor in peace.

One of the most important encyclicals of our time is *Mater et magistra,* Pope John XXIII's great statement of Christian social teaching in the light of the urgent problems of the mid-twentieth century. This encyclical is not only for specialists, political economists, and sociologists. It is for every man of good will and it especially concerns every member of Christ, because we are all deeply involved in the social, economic, and political problems of our time. The Christian cannot separate his life of faith from the real world of work and struggle in which he lives. His life in Christ will inevitably be affected by his attitude toward such problems as nuclear war, the race question, the growth of new nations, and the whole crucial struggle between the communist and noncommunist worlds.

Therefore it can never be sufficient for him to lead a "Christian life" that is confined, in practice, to the pews of the parish Church and to a few prayers in the home, without regard for these acute problems which affect millions of human beings and which call into question not only the future of man's civilization but even perhaps the very survival of the human race itself. We are all implicated in these tremendous problems, and we are obliged not only by our vocation as Christians but even by our human nature itself to cooperate in the great effort to solve them with equity and efficiency.

Pope John has said: "Although the Holy Church has the special task of sanctifying souls and making them participants in the goods of the supernatural order, she is also solicitous for the exigencies of the daily life of men, not merely those concerning the nourishment of the body and the material conditions of life, but also those that concern prosperity and culture in all its many aspects and stages. . . ."

Whatever is the concern of the Church is also the concern of every member of the Church, not only of the hierarchy and clergy. Indeed, the economic questions discussed in *Mater et magistra* come under the special competency of the Christian layman, the citizen, the manufacturer, the farmer, the politician, and the man of business. When these ordinary human activities are carried out in a Christian way, that is to say in full accordance with the natural order established by God and clarified by the teaching and legislation of the Church, then they cannot help but contribute to the holiness and salvation of those who participate in them.

The Church teaches us that work is one of the fundamental human activities which can help man to be holy. First of all, work should rightly be "not a commodity but an expression of the human person." This phrase of *Mater et magistra* has profound significance. Our time, our skill, our energy are not simply commodities which we put on sale. If we assume that they are, then we will inevitably concentrate more on selling our talents than on using them in a fruitful and satisfying manner. Our capacities and gifts will become subservient to our main purpose: "making money." But this is a perversion of the natural order, in which the productive use of human talents in good and fruitful work should normally be a deeply human and satisfying activity in itself, not only bringing in a just wage and contributing to the support of a family, but also fulfilling certain fundamental spiritual and psychological needs of the human person. In a disordered social setting work loses this basically healthy character, and becomes frustrating or irrational.

When work is mere thoughtless drudgery, slavery to a machine or to some other of the countless mechanical routines of modern life, undertaken only in view of a wage, then naturally the mind and system of the worker react against this irrationality and disorder. On the one hand, meaningful activity is sought in some sort of tension-releasing recreation that relieves the tedium of one's daily job. On the other, a person with spiritual aspirations may tend more and more to escape from his monotonous and futile work-routines into a separate spiritual realm in which he tries to find comfort in prayer and communion with a God who has emphatically nothing to do with the world of machines.

However, there is still another unfortunate possibility, and one that is by no means unfrequent. This seriously aggravates the disorder. One can plunge entirely into the activity of making money as an end in itself. One can become so absorbed in the rituals and complexities of business, so deeply involved in the activity of planning and making deals, that everything else loses its meaning. Home-life takes second (or third) place, the family loses its significance, personal relationships become ambivalent and frustrating if they interfere with the main object of one's life which is to make money. Life becomes artificial, tense, and false. The genuine human dimensions shrivel up. In order to keep up the pace and cope with the contradictions that one has built into his own existence, he may resort to alcohol, or tranquilizers—or both. In such an atmosphere true spirituality becomes an almost total impossibility. At best religion remains a veneer, an outward form, or a vague, disquieting velleity: one of those many things that one will get around to "later."

The implications of Christian social teaching in the realm of work are then deep and far reaching. *Mater et magistra* combats the unnatural division that splits modern man and his life down the middle. Work must once again become spiritually meaningful and humanly satisfying. The encyclical says:

"We should not create an artificial opposition between the perfection of our own being and our active presence in the world; as if a man could not perfect himself except by putting aside all temporal activity, and that wherever such action is done a man is inevitably led to compromise his personal dignity as a human being and as a believer. . . . It is perfectly in keeping with the plan of divine providence that each one develop and perfect himself through his daily work, which for almost all human beings is of a temporal nature."

However, it would be a wrong interpretation of this passage from *Mater et magistra* if one were to conclude that all it means is that the worker must look at his work "in a spiritual light." This is not just a repetition of the familiar advice to "offer it up" and "purify our intentions." This paragraph must be read in the context of the whole encyclical which demands that the true objective nature of work as a free expression of human dignity and a creative activity of the human person should be restored by a Christian renewal in society itself. In other words, it implies an admission that in fact a great deal of work now done by men, whether in labor, in business, or in the professions, has a somewhat less than human character. This disorder cannot be rectified merely by an interior, subjective adjustment, however spiritual.

The task of restoring work to its proper place in the Christian life is then more than a personal, interior project for the individual. It is a cooperative and objective obligation of the Church and of human society. The individual Christian will do more to "sanctify" his work by becoming intelligently concerned with social order and with effective political means to improve social conditions, than he will ever be able to do by merely interior and personal spiritual efforts to overcome the tedium and meaninglessness of a subhuman battle for money. It goes without saying that this task is enormous. It has almost endless ramifications. They lead in all directions, into politics, economics, business, and everything that seriously affects the life of the nation and the international community.

We are faced on all sides with disorder, with confusion, with ever aggravated tensions, with ever new ruptures in the body of an agonized society. Where can one begin to cope with the urgent problem of the Christian renewal of modern society?

Mater et magistra gives one fundamental theological principle on which rests the Church's teaching of the spiritual value of work. Since the Word of God became Incarnate, the common task of the human race to build a just and truly productive society can be endowed with a more than human character. It takes on something of the nature of a supernatural mission, a prolongation of the work begun by Christ in his historical existence. We read in the encyclical:

"When one carries on his proper activity, even if it be of a temporal nature, in union with Jesus the Divine Redeemer, every work becomes a continuation of his work and is penetrated with redemptive power. . . . It thus becomes a work which contributes to one's own personal supernatural perfection and helps to extend to others the fruits of the Redemption, and leavens with the ferment of the Gospel the civilization in which one lives and works."

However this will not really be effective unless our work is seen as a service to humanity. To offer such service means to understand and appreciate all that is valuable to man in social order, culture, and civilization. This implies an outlook that can best be qualified as humanism.

HOLINESS AND HUMANISM

To assert a need for "humanism" in Christian life may sound provocative and vaguely heretical to those Christians who have trained themselves to respond negatively to the shock of this often ambiguous word. Can humanism have anything to do with holiness? Are not the two radically opposed to one another, as God and man are opposed? Do we not have to choose the divine and reject the human? Is not the espousal of human values the mark of those who have rejected God? Though there have been and perhaps still are "Christian humanists," have these not been men who were lured by a false optimism to compromise their faith in a perilous dialogue with the "world"?

One may answer with the words of St. John's Gospel: "The Word was made flesh and dwelt amongst us." If the Word of God assumed a human nature and became a man, in all things like other men except sin, if he gave his life to unite the human race to God in his Mystical Body, then surely there must be an authentic humanism which is not only acceptable to Christians but is essential to the Christian mystery itself. This humanism is obviously not a glorification of the passions, of the flesh, of sinful tendencies, of a perverse and disordered libertarianism, of disobedience. But it must be the full acceptance of those values which are essential to man as he was created by God, those values which God himself has willed to preserve, rescue, and restore to their rightful order by taking them to himself in Christ.

In defending the natural law, the civic rights of men,

the rights of human reason, the cultural values of diverse civilizations, scientific study and technics, medicine, political science and a thousand other good things in the natural order, the Church is expressing her profoundly Christian humanism, or, in other words, her concern for man in all his wholeness and integrity as a creature and as the image of God, destined for the contemplation of absolute truth and beauty in heaven.

The salvation of man does not mean that he must divest himself of all that is human: that he must discard his reason, his love of beauty, his desire for friendship, his need for human affection, his reliance on protection, order, and justice in society, his need to work and eat and sleep.

A Christianity that despises these fundamental needs of man is not truly worthy of the name. And doubtless there is no one who would claim that the Church should not be concerned about such matters. But the trouble is that while all Christians would readily agree that "humanism" in this good sense is a matter of general or official concern, few will see that it is of vital concern to them personally. In other words, it is very important to realize that Christian humanism is not a luxury which the Church grudgingly permits to a few esthetes and social reformers, but a necessity in the life of every Christian. There is no genuine holiness without this dimension of human and social concern. It is not enough to contribute tax-deductible sums to various "charities." We are obliged to take an active part in the solution of urgent problems affecting the whole of our society and of our world.

If this statement sounds extreme, then let us listen to Pope John XXIII. He says in *Mater et magistra*:

"We reaffirm strongly that Christian social doctrine is an integral part of the Christian conception of life. . . .

"Our beloved sons, the laity, can greatly contribute [to the diffusion of this doctrine] by knowing [it] and making their actions conform to it, by zealously striving to make others understand it . . . A social doctrine has to be translated into reality and not just formulated. This is particularly true of the Christian social doctrine whose light is truth, its objective, justice, and its driving force, love. . . .

"Christian education should be complete in extending itself to every kind of obligation, hence it should strive to implant and foster among the faithful an awareness of the obligation to carry on in a Christian manner their economic and social activities."

The teaching of the modern popes is concerned especially with the human condition of man in the technological age. Pope Pius XI (quoted in *Mater et magistra*), pointed to the dehumanization of man in industrial society, in which by a significant contradiction human labor, which should serve the good of man, became "an instrument of strange perversion: for, dead matter leaves the factory ennobled and transformed, where men are corrupted and degraded" (*Quadragesimo anno*). Hence the Church is obligated to protect man against the encroachment of a secularized society on his human dignity. She should defend him against a world-view in which money and power are held to be of greater importance than man himself.

The task of the Christian is then not simply to concern himself with social justice, with political order and fair trade practices. It goes much deeper than that. It is a question of the very structure of society and of man's cultural heritage. The task of each Christian today is to help defend and restore the basic human values without which grace and spirituality will have little practical meaning in the life of man.

It is essential to recognize the danger to human values that exists in that very technology, which promises man abundance, leisure, and, indeed, an earthly paradise. The inherent contradiction of a society capable of producing the greatest affluence and yet at the same time geared for an all-out race toward global suicide, is succinctly pointed out by John XXIII in *Mater et magistra*. He concludes:

"Today the Church is confronted with an immense task: that of giving a human and Christian note to modern civilization; a note that is required and almost asked by that civilization itself for its further development and even for its continued existence."

PRACTICAL PROBLEMS

In such a situation it is no longer permissible for Christians seriously and honestly to devote themselves to a spirituality of evasion, a cult of other worldliness that refuses to take account of the *inescapable implication of all men* in the problems and responsibilities of the nuclear age. No matter what may be the alleged motive for this abdication, it cannot be acceptable to God, and it cannot therefore contribute to Christian holiness. Indifference and callousness can no longer mask as "recollection," and cowardly withdrawal may not allege the excuse that it is a sacrifice and an act of worship. Passivity is no longer to be counted as "faith" or "abandonment." Lack of interest in the desperate fate of man is a sign of culpable insensitivity, a deplorable incapacity to love! It cannot in any sense claim to be Christian. It is not even genuinely human.

Yet it is not easy to orient oneself intelligently in the turmoil of modern affairs about which the directives of the Church are general and must necessarily remain somewhat vague until they are put into action by energetic interpretation and leadership in concrete cases. Hence it is unfortunately all too true that countless Christians, with all the good will in the world, find it almost impossible to get sufficient information and adequate directives to play a significant part in the great issues of the time, such as for instance the question of world peace.

The practical social problems of our time are innumerable, and one who seeks to fulfil his obligations of conscience in this matter necessarily runs many risks. Nevertheless, the risks must be taken, and there is no virtue in inertia or in a despondent and passive "prudence" which refuses to move until the whole Church, from the Papal Curia on down, moves first. Pope John XXIII has stated in the clearest terms that Christian perfection has nothing to do with negativism and withdrawal. The temporal problems of our time are doubtless not only distracting but positively maddening. Yet they must be faced. Pope John says:

> It would be an error if our sons,
> especially the laity,
> should consider it more prudent
> to lessen their personal Christian commitment
> to the world:
> rather should they renew and increase it.

Naturally, the duties of various states of life remain intact. The field of politics and economics, of business and industry is for the layman, not for the priest and religious. The initiatives of a Jesuit priest in contemporary affairs will certainly be more developed than those of a Carmelite nun. In demanding that all recognize their obligation to interest themselves in the problems of our time and take an active part in solving them, the pope was not saying that all should abandon their state of life and go into politics. But he is saying that even the religious must take a deeper view of his own life, and he must see it clearly in relation to the poverty of the greater part of the human race, the threat of social upheaval, and above all, the threat of all-out nuclear war. To these things no Christian can remain indifferent, because they are not just political or economic problems: they are symptoms of a spiritual sickness so universal and so deep rooted that it threatens the very existence of the human race.

However, the layman, the priest, and the religious will all approach these problems in characteristically different ways. Traditionally, the priest and the religious who have given themselves to God and have "renounced the world," dedicate themselves to special spiritual tasks in the world. They have, or should have, given up political office, military life, careers in business, medicine, law, and so forth. The purpose of this renunciation is to free them for urgent spiritual missions which they alone can perform. In their case it is true that serious involvement in purely temporal affairs does by its nature constitute an obstacle to the perfection of their state of life. Exceptions of course can always arise.

One of the sources of trouble and confusion in the lives of religious and priests, as well as of lay-people, is the fact that over the centuries the theoretical boundaries between states and offices of Christian life have been to some extent lost in practice.

In the early Middle Ages, prelates and priests, not to mention monks with their abbots, often assumed the highest political responsibilities or engaged in military campaigns to protect their rights or even to fight for secular authorities. When the only educated men in society were the clerks, or *clerici*, it was natural for practically all the professions to be exercised by the clergy. Obviously, in such a situation, the clergy played a leading part in government. History shows us many instructive examples of this development, in which gradually the clergy assumed functions that belonged properly to the laity. Though of course in most nations today the clergy do not actually participate in government, business, and law, within the Church the situation has remained what it was centuries ago. It is quite taken for granted that even the material affairs of the Church are in the hands of clerics or religious.

Hence the clergy and religious are overburdened with tasks and functions many of which are concerned with business and purely temporal matters. Such responsibilities might conceivably be undertaken, at least in part, by lay persons. As a matter of fact, when we consider the problem of vocations in the active religious life, it is hardly surprising that young people will think twice before embracing a state of life in which they may well have to carry out the work of lay persons *in addition to* the work and observances of religious, in such a way that they have no assurance of acquitting themselves properly of either responsibility. Indeed, it may seem reasonable to hold back from such a commitment when they think they will have the difficulties and burdens of both kinds of life, without all the corresponding advantages of the religious state.

A corollary of this is that since religious are burdened with secular tasks they acquire in some sense a "right" to secular relaxations. Or at least this seems to be one of the ways in which the problem is met. But is this satisfactory? Something must give place to these recreations, and obviously this means encroaching not only on the formal "religious exercises" of the community but also on the leisure essential for the spiritual life of the individual religious: that spiritual life which he or she is supposed to be effectively combining with his work. Whatever may be said about this, and certainly there are many points both for and against it, we can see that when religious are habitually involved in deeply engrossing secular occupations, their religious life must inevitably suffer.

But if this is the case, they are not able to fulfil their true function in the Church. It is not to such people that one should address, without further qualification, the advice to consider their work itself as a spiritual activity. One must distinguish. The work that is proper to their rule and constitutions, within the limits foreseen by the Church for them, will indeed sanctify them. It retains a sacred character. But when in addition to what is really theirs, they undertake innumerable tasks that should be done by somebody else, profane jobs which involve ever increasing demands on their time and ever new compromises with the spirit of their vocation, then a serious adjustment is called for. This adjustment is not something that can be effected by the good will of the individual religious. It is not a matter of good intentions and personal piety, but of reform.

Lay people can certainly help more and more in work that is now done by religious, in education, administration of institutions, nursing, journalism, the apostolate, the missions and so on. They can assume responsibilities which will leave the clergy free for a more intense and fruitful ministry.

But this is a digression. The point at issue is that all Christians, lay people, religious and priests, must play a constructive and positive part in the world of our time. Even contemplatives, insofar as they have the right and the obligation to vote, must have an intelligent grasp of what is going on in the world. Serious objective information on the state of the world can and should contribute to their spiritual life by making them aware of the perils that face the Body of Christ. But they must surely be able to take a wiser and more profound view than that which is given by the mass media. In fact, this is important for all Christians. One of the great problems of our time is *the lack of reliable and serious information and of sound perspective* in political and social affairs. Once again, the case of nuclear warfare and the attendant political problems, presents itself as the most serious of all. Here we have an issue of supreme importance in which the most vital facts are secret and in which crucial developments are rarely presented to the public in a clear, unbiased form.

This brings us to one more grave problem. The Christian who is misinformed; who is subject to the demagoguery of extremists in the press, on the radio or on TV, and who is perhaps to some extent temperamentally inclined to associate himself with fanatical groups in politics, can do an enormous amount of harm to society, to the Church and to himself. With sincere intentions of serving the cause of Christ he may cooperate in follies and injustices of disastrous magnitude.

It is therefore vitally important for the Catholic to control his zeal and moderate his enthusiasm for particular causes, until he can accurately estimate where these tendencies may ultimately lead. Prudence is not passivity, and caution is not cowardice. Impetuous and violent action must not be regarded as *ipso facto* heroic. We must learn to cultivate a sound judgment in affairs that affect the very destiny of the human race. Let us above all listen to the wise directives of the Church, and especially those of the Holy Father. They have a direct bearing not only on political life, but on the whole question of Christian holiness, and indeed on the basic problem of salvation itself.

And now, returning to the theme of holiness. Remember that in Christian tradition, renunciation, sacrifice, and generous self-denial are essential to sanctity. It is true that often the laity have been confused by the idea that they could only become holy by practicing austerities and mortifications appropriate to convent life. This is not true, and it is another example of the confusion of borderlines between the religious and the lay states. Nevertheless, the abnegation of the religious and of the lay person is the same insofar as it tends to one and the same end. Its purpose is to *liberate the mind and will* so that all the energies of body and spirit can be dedicated to God in a way appropriate to one's particular state.

ABNEGATION AND HOLINESS

To deny ourselves in the fullest sense is to renounce not only what we have but also what we are—to live not according to our own desire and our own judgment but according to God's will for us. Thus Christian abnegation will reach into the most intimate depths of our being.

Religious bind themselves by vow to perform certain exterior acts of discipline and worship which enable them more simply and directly to reach the perfection of charity. "If thou wilt be perfect, go, sell what thou hast, and give to the poor, and thou shalt have treasure in heaven; and come, follow me" (Mt. 19:21). In addition to the general obligation imposed on all to tend to the perfect love of God, the religious is also obliged to fulfill these special obligations which he has vowed. They are given him for a purpose: that he may grow interiorly in love and in union with Christ. This interior development of love is true growth in perfection. Hence the religious must make use of the means offered him by his state to renounce "the world," to live more perfectly "according to the spirit," and grow in union with God.

The layman certainly does not have all the spiritual advantages that are offered by the religious state. But let us not forget that the lay state has advantages and indeed sacrifices of its own. Religious vows are by no means the only form of heroism open to the Christian who is seeking holiness. The obligations of marriage are in fact often no less difficult than those of the cloister. Marriage is a sacrament, hence the married life is especially sanctified by sacramental grace. This sacramental grace raises married love to a spiritual plane, and hence it is not an obstacle to union with Christ. If it is seen in a spirit of faith it becomes an opportunity to grow in holiness, by the gift of oneself in simplicity and love.

Hence we must not imagine that married life is "life in the flesh" and religious life alone is "life in the spirit." The married life is a truly spiritual vocation, though in many ways it is accidentally rendered difficult by the fact that married people do not recognize their spiritual opportunities and often find no one to guide them in the right direction.

It is certainly tragic that married Christians should imagine themselves somehow debarred from lives of holiness and perfection just because they find it difficult or impossible to imitate the austerities, the devotions, and the spiritual practices of religious.

On the contrary, they should rejoice in the fact that the Church has left them free in all these matters to find what suits their own needs best. Let them read the New Testament and imitate the spirit of those first Christians who ate together "breaking their bread in joy and simplicity of heart" (Acts 2:46–47). Let them immerse themselves in the liturgical life of the Church, and draw from her Eucharistic worship all the strength they need to live in love and forget themselves.

The way of holiness is a way of confidence and love. The true Christian lives "in the Spirit" and drinks at every moment from the hidden fountains of divine grace, without being obsessed with any special need for complicated and marginal practices. He is concerned above all with essentials—with frequent moments of simple prayer and faith; attention to the presence of God; loving submission to the divine will in all things, especially in his duties of state; and above all the love of his neighbor and brother in Christ.

Abnegation will, however, never be absent. The Christian must lead a life of often bitter sacrifice. The constant effort to control passionate and selfish reactions, to submit to the demands of love, requires perpetual and unremitting sacrifice.

"Therefore, brethen, we are debtors, not to the flesh, that we should live according to the flesh, for if you live according to the flesh you will die; but if by the spirit you put to death the deeds of the flesh, you will live.

"For whoever are led by the Spirit of God, they are the sons of God. Now you have not received a spirit of bondage so as to be again in fear, but you have received a spirit of adoption as sons, by virtue of which we cry, 'Abba! Father!' The Spirit himself gives testimony to our spirit that we are sons of God. But if we are sons, we are heirs also; heirs indeed of God and joint heirs with Christ, provided, however, we suffer with him that we may also be glorified with him" (Rom. 8:12–17).

"But the fruit of the Spirit is: charity, joy, peace, patience, kindness, goodness, faith, modesty, continency. Against such things there is no law. And they who belong to Christ have crucified their flesh with its passions and desires. If we live by the Spirit, by the Spirit let us also walk. Let us not become desirous of vainglory, provoking one another, envying one another" (Gal. 5:22–25).

St. Thomas, however, makes it quite clear that absolute perfection is impossible in the present life. The perfection to which we must tend is the highest and most complete, *but this is achieved only in heaven*. In heaven our love will always actually and totally be directed to God. Such perfection is not possible on earth. The perfection that can be attained in this life is that which excludes everything that is opposed to the love of God:

a) The exclusion of all mortal sin—and this comes under the commandments.

b) The removal of impediments to true love—and this comes under the counsels.

St. Thomas was here referring to the life of religious

vows; but certainly the evangelical counsels are not excluded from the life of the Christian layman. He too can consider in what ways he can, at least by living in a spirit of poverty for example, go beyond the level of the commandments and devote his life to God in a way that permits of closer attention to his presence and a more complete union with his holy will.

Some of the early desert fathers believed that a quasi absolute perfection could be attained in this life, by ascetic discipline. Cassian believed this was possible. St. Jerome at first believed it also, but afterward renounced the opinion—and like St. Thomas decided that we can be only *relatively* perfect in the present life. We will never be without some semideliberate faults of weakness. This is true even of the saints, who all retained their frailties and human limitations.

It is a paradox of monastic history that the super-human ideal of perfect conquest of all the passions in the present life is a pagan rather than a Christian concept; and therefore is an ideal of "flesh" rather than of the "spirit." In Christian sanctity, a certain human weakness and imperfection are altogether compatible with the perfect love of God, as long as one acquires humility from the experience of his own wretchedness and thus learns to place an ever more total and perfect trust in the grace of God. St. Paul is a classic example:

"And lest the greatness of the revelations should puff me up, there was given me a thorn for the flesh, a messenger of Satan, to buffet me. Concerning this I thrice besought the Lord that it might leave me. And he has said to me, My grace is sufficient for thee, for strength is made perfect in weakness.' Gladly therefore I will glory in my infirmities, that the strength of Christ may dwell in me. Wherefore I am satisfied, for Christ's sake, with infirmities, with insults, with hardships, with persecutions, with distresses. For when I am weak, then I am strong" (2 Cor. 12:7–10).

This does not mean that the Christian cannot attain to a very real and relatively perfect peace even in the present life. Certainly we all can and must struggle to attain tranquillity of heart and liberate ourselves from inordinate passion. Without this interior peace we cannot truly come to know God and enjoy the familiarity with him which is proper to us as sons.

Peace, however, is not to be obtained by brute force and by the violent, despotic suppression of our appetites. Peace is not the work of force but the fruit of love. And love means submission to Christ, docile subjection to his Spirit. True peace is the work of God's mercy and not of man's will. When we yield ourselves to him in love, his presence itself appeases our desires and quiets the rebellious passions. And if at times there are storms in our hearts, if God appears to be sleeping, we can still have deep peace in the midst of conflict, if we really trust him. And indeed we must learn that he allows conflict precisely in order to purify our hearts, test our patience, and thus strengthen our spiritual peace.

The perfection of Christian abnegation paradoxically includes even the renunciation of a certain inordinate pleasure in our own virtue and ascetic prowess (if any). The saints are not arrogant and self-assured characters whose virtues have made them rich and powerful in the spiritual order. Rather they are like Jeremias men who fully realize their poverty before God:

I am the man that see my poverty by the rod of his indignation.
He hath led me, and brought me into darkness, and not into light.
Only against me he hath turned, and turned again his hand all the day.
My skin and my flesh he hath made old, he hath broken my bones.

He hath built round about me, and he hath compassed me with gall and labor.

．　　　．　　　．　　　．　　　．　　　．

He hath turned aside my paths, and hath broken me in pieces, he hath made me desolate.
He hath bent his bow, and set me as a mark for his arrows.
He hath shot into my reins the daughters of his quiver.
I am made a derision to all my people, their song all the day long.
He hath filled me with bitterness, he hath inebriated me with wormwood.
And he hath broken my teeth one by one, he hath fed me with ashes.
And my soul is removed far off from peace, I have forgotten good things.

．　　　．　　　．　　　．　　　．　　　．

I will be mindful and remember, and my soul shall languish within me.
These things I shall think over in my heart, and therefore will I hope.
The mercies of the Lord that we are not consumed: because his commiserations have not failed.
They are new every morning, great is thy faithfulness.
The Lord is my portion, said my soul: therefore will I wait for him.
The Lord is good to them that hope in him, to the soul that seeketh him.
It is good to wait with silence for the salvation of God.
Lamentations 3:1–5, 11–17, 20–26.

This is the true purpose of abnegation—not simply to bring peace of heart as the reward for detachment, but to lead to that interior tribulation of the spiritual night in which one's poverty becomes perfect in the depths of the soul, one's chastity becomes virginity of intellect and of spirit, and one's obedience is a direct dependence on the Holy Spirit at every moment of one's life. This sublime life in the spirit of the evangelical counsels is accessible to all who are holy, whether in religion or out of it.

St. Thomas says: "Those who are perfect in life are *said to offend in many things by venial sins which flow from the weakness of this present life.*" He adds: "It is sufficient that love be directed commonly and universally to all men as well as to God, and habitually to individuals around us, according to dispositions. Perfect fraternal charity is measured not only by the fact that it excludes everything contrary to charity, but also by the fact that it extends even to strangers and enemies, and that it goes to great lengths to sacrifice itself for them, even to the point of dying for them."

What then, in résumé, is the perfection possible to us in the present life? Not a perfection in which we actually and at every moment tend directly to God—not even a perfection in which we can avoid all semideliberate venial sin. What then?

We love God with our whole heart and our whole mind and our whole soul and all our strength when all our thoughts, desires, and actions are directed *at least virtually* to him, and when we strive as far as possible to grow in the purity of our love and in the totality of our consecration. This implies sincere fidelity to one's obligations and generous response to all the demands of love in one's life. But beyond that it means a total faith in God and as far as possible complete abandonment to his merciful providence and love.

CONCLUSION

Jesus is our sanctity and our way to the Father. "No man cometh to the Father but by me" (Jn. 14:6). "I am the way, the truth, and the life" (Jn. 14:6). "I am the vine, you are the branches . . . abide in me and I in you" (Jn. 15:4–5). How do we abide in Him? By love . . . "Abide in my love" (Jn. 15:9).

How do we abide in Christ and please the Father? By doing the Father's will as Jesus did, in loving attention and submission to the Holy Spirit. "In this is my Father glorified that you bring forth very much fruit and become my disciples. . . . If you keep my commandments you shall abide in my love. . . . If you love me keep my commandments. . . . He that hath my commandments and keepeth them, he it is that loveth me. . . . He that loveth me not, keepeth not my words . . ." (Jn. 14 and 15).

The will of Christ is above all that we love one another. "A new commandment I give you, that you love one another as I have loved you . . . By this shall all men know that you are my disciples, if you have love one for another" (Jn. 13:34–35).

It is true that Christian sanctity is the sanctity of Christ in us: but this does not mean that the Holy Spirit will do his work in us while we remain completely passive and inert. There is no spiritual life without persistent struggle and interior conflict. This conflict is all the more difficult to wage because it is hidden, mysterious, and sometimes almost impossible to understand. Every serious Christian is willing to make a few initial sacrifices. It is not hard to make a good start. But it is hard to continue, to carry on the work begun, and to persevere in it through many years until the end. The effort of faith is too great, the tax on our weak love is too enormous: or at least we fear that it will become so. We do not understand the meaning of the cross and the seriousness of our vocation to die with Christ in order to rise with him to a new life. It is perfectly true that we die with him in baptism and rise from the dead: but this is only the beginning of a series of deaths and resurrections. We are not "converted" only once in our life but many times, and this endless series of large and small "conversions," inner revolutions, leads finally to our transformation in Christ. But while we may have the generosity to undergo one or two such upheavals, we cannot face the necessity of further and greater rendings of our inner self, without which we cannot finally become free.

Paradoxically, then, though Christ himself accomplishes the work of our sanctification, the more he does so the more it tends to cost us. The further we advance the more he tends to take away our own strength and deprive us of our own human and natural resources, so that in the end we find ourselves in complete poverty and darkness. This is the situation that we find most terrible, and it is against this that we rebel. For the strange, sanctifying mystery of Christ's death in us, we substitute the more familiar and comforting routine of our own activity: we abandon his will and take refuge in the more trivial, but more "satisfying," procedures which interest us and enable us to be interesting in the eyes of others. We think that in this way we can find peace, and make our lives fruitful: but we delude ourselves, and our activity turns out to be spiritually sterile.

Cardinal Newman—who certainly knew the bitterness and irony of the cross—lived by the maxim: "holiness before peace." This maxim is good for anyone who wants to remember the full seriousness of the Christian life. If we seek holiness, then peace will be taken care of in good time. Our Lord, who came to bring "not peace but the sword" also promised a peace that the world cannot give. We, insofar as we rely on our own anxious efforts, are of this world. We are not capable of producing such peace by our own efforts. We can only find it when we have, in some sense, renounced peace and forgotten about it.

However, let us not overemphasize the element of darkness and trial in the Christian life. For the believing Christian, darkness becomes filled with spiritual light and faith receives a new dimension—the dimension of understanding and wisdom. "Blessed are the clean of heart, for they shall *see* God" (Mt. 5:8). The perfect Christian is therefore not one who is necessarily impeccable and beyond all moral weakness; but he is one who, because his eyes are enlightened to know the full dimensions of the mercy of Christ, is no longer troubled by the sorrows and frailties of this present life. His confidence in God is perfect, because he now *"knows,"* so to speak, by experience that God cannot fail him (and yet this knowledge is simply a new dimension of loyal faith). He responds to the mercy of God with perfect trust. "Nay, we are confident even over our afflictions, knowing well that affliction gives rise to endurance, and endurance gives proof of our faith and a proved faith gives ground for hope. *Nor does this hope delude us;* the love of God has been formed forth in our hearts by the Holy Spirit whom we have received" (Rom. 5:2–5). As Clement of Alexandria says, such perfect Christians, perfect in hope and in the knowledge of divine mercy, are always present to God in prayer for even when they are not explicitly praying they are seeking him and relying on his grace alone. Not only that, but since they seek only God's will, every petition of their hearts, whether spoken or unspoken, is granted by God (*Stromata vii.* 7. 41). For such men, true lovers of God, all things, whether they appear good or evil, are in actuality good. All things manifest the loving mercy of God. All things enable them to grow in love. All events serve to unite them closer to God. For such men *obstacles no longer exist.* God has turned even obstacles into means to their ends, which are also his own. This is the meaning of "spiritual perfection," and it is attained not by those who have superhuman strength but by those who, though weak and defective in themselves, trust perfectly in the love of God.

The final step on the way to holiness in Christ is then to completely abandon ourselves with confident joy to the apparent madness of the cross. "The word of the cross to them indeed that perish is foolishness, but to them that are saved, that is to us, it is the power of God" (1 Cor. 1:18). This madness, the folly of abandoning all concern for ourselves both in the material and in the spiritual order, that we may entrust ourselves to Christ, means a kind of death to our temporal selves. It is a twisting, a letting go, an act of total abandonment. But it is also a final break-through into joy. The ability to make this act, to let go, to plunge into our own emptiness and there find the freedom of Christ in all fullness—this is inaccessible to all our merely human efforts and plans. We cannot do it by relaxing or by striving, by thinking or not thinking, by acting or not acting. The only answer is perfect faith, exultant hope, transformed by a completely spiritual love of Christ. This is a pure gift of his: but we can dispose ourselves to receive it by fortitude, humility, patience, and, above all, by simple fidelity to his will in every circumstance of our ordinary life.